Old People
As People

Little, Brown Series on Gerontology

Series Editors

Jon Hendricks
and
Robert Kastenbaum

Published

Donald E. Gelfand
*Aging: The Ethnic
Factor*

Jennie Keith
*Old People
As People: Social
and Cultural
Influences on
Aging and Old Age*

Theodore H. Koff
*Long-Term Care:
An Approach
to Serving the Frail
Elderly*

Forthcoming
Titles

W. Andrew Achenbaum
*Aging: History
and Ideology*

Linda M. Breytspraak
*The Development
of Self in Later Life*

Carroll Estes
*Political Economy,
Health, and Aging*

Charles Harris et al.
*Applied Research
In Aging*

C. Davis Hendricks
Law and Aging

John L. Horn
*Aging and
Adult
Development
of Cognitive
Functions*

John F. Myles
*Political Economy
of Pensions*

Martha Storandt
*Counseling
and Psychotherapy*

Albert J. E. Wilson III
*Social Services
For Older Persons*

Old People As People

Social and Cultural Influences on Aging and Old Age

Jennie Keith
Swarthmore College

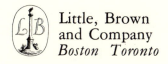

Little, Brown
and Company
Boston Toronto

Library of Congress Cataloging in Publication Data

Keith, Jennie.
  Old people as people.

  (Little, Brown series on gerontology)
  Bibliography: p. 120
  Includes index.
  1. Aging—Social aspects. 2. Old Age—Social
aspects. I. Title. II. Series.
HQ1061.K398   305.2'6   82-114
ISBN 0-316-48631-0   AACR2
ISBN 0-316-48632-9 (pbk.)

Library of Congress Catalog Card No. 82-114

ISBN 0-316-486310
ISBN 0-316-486329 (pbk.)

9 8 7 6 5 4 3 2 1

HAL

Published simultaneously in Canada
by Little, Brown & Company (Canada) Limited

Printed in the United States of America

For Fitz

Foreword to Series

Where is it? In each of the billions of cells in our bodies? Or in our minds? Then, again, perhaps it is something that happens *between* people. Ought we not also take a look at the marketplace as well? And at the values expressed through our cultural institutions? Undoubtedly, the answer lies in all these factors—and more. The phenomenon of aging takes place within our bodies, in our minds, between ourselves and others, and in culturally defined patterns.

The study and analysis of aging—a burgeoning field—is deserving of an integrated spectrum approach. Now, Little, Brown and Company offers such a perspective, one designed to respond to the diversity and complexity of the subject matter and to individualized instructional needs. The Little, Brown Series on Gerontology provides a series of succinct and readable books that encompass a wide variety of topics and concerns. Each volume, written by a highly qualified gerontologist, will provide a degree of precision and specificity not available in a general text whose coverage, expertise and interest level cannot help but be uneven. While the scope of the gerontology series is indeed broad, individual volumes provide accurate, up-to-date presentations unmatched in the literature of gerontology.

The Little, Brown Series on Gerontology:

—provides a comprehensive overview
—explores emerging challenges and extends the frontiers of knowledge
—is organically interrelated via cross-cutting themes
—consists of individual volumes prepared by the most qualified experts

—offers maximum flexibility as teaching materials

—insures manageable length without sacrificing concepts, facts, methods, or issues

With the Little, Brown Series on Gerontology now becoming available, instructors can select the texts most desirable for their individual courses. Practitioners and other professionals will also find the foundations necessary to remain abreast of their own particular areas. No doubt, students too will respond to the knowledge and enthusiasm of gerontologists writing about only those topics they know and care most about.

Little, Brown and Company and the editors are pleased to provide a series that not only looks at conceptual and theoretical questions but squarely addresses the most critical and applied concerns of the 1980s. Knowledge without action is unacceptable. The reverse is no better.

As the list of volumes makes clear, some books focus primarily on research and theoretical concerns, others on the applied; by this two-sided approach they draw upon the most significant and dependable thinking available. It is hoped that they will serve as a wellspring for developments in years to come.

Preface

This book is written in response to a question that I am asked whenever I talk about my research with older people. Forms and tones of voice vary, but the essential query is always the same: Aren't you saying that old people are just like everybody else? The question is asked sometimes with surprise, sometimes with disappointment, sometimes with obvious annoyance. My answer is as persistent as the question: Yes, old people are people just like everybody else. Since what was a starting premise to me turns out to be a startling conclusion to others, I think it's time to develop the dialogue into a book. *Old People As People* therefore has as both origin and goal an exploration of the ways in which older people are human, i.e., both constrained and liberated by the social and cultural contexts in which they age and are old. It also tries to discover why the humanity of old people should surprise, disappoint, or annoy members of our own particular social and cultural context.

I am very grateful to Joe Hendricks for editorial critique and encouragement far beyond the call of duty, to my students and audiences for pressing me to make more orderly and explicit my thinking about old age, and to my entire expanded family for support of all kinds during the writing.

Contents

Chapter

1

Old Age in Cross-Cultural Perspective

"Is that really anthropology?" is the question I'm most often asked about my research with older people. Don't anthropologists go to study exotic societies and bring back reports about unknown customs and views of the world? My answer to both questions is yes—but there's no contradiction. Old people are an exotic group in most industrial societies because we make them outsiders, keep them at a distance, and so know very little about them. This is in one way understandable, and in another way a rather remarkable psychological feat.

Our lack of knowledge about old people is understandable from the point of view that the situation of the elderly in modern societies is unknown in a profound sense: they occupy a space in the life course that is new territory in human experience. Extended life, better health, and retirement laws have created a new interval between work and death; and the people who occupy it now are pioneers who must explore and define the potential of a new territory for human habitation. Old age itself is in evolutionary terms characteristically human: old individuals are rare among other primate groups such as apes or monkeys (Dolhinow forthcoming). Like other human specialties, presence of numerous old people in human communities is, however, foreshadowed in the behavior of other primates. Old female macaque and langur monkeys defend and care for their young relatives to the extent that a grandmother may be a survival asset. Old monkeys also ease crises through their knowledge of the environment, e.g., by leading others to a formerly used water hole during a drought (Hrdy 1981). The great proportion of human culture that must be learned may have intensified the value of old people both as caretakers during our extended human childhood, and as living archives of experience (Katz 1978).

The remarkable psychological feat is that so many of us are able to *maintain* a sense of distance from old people. Yes, they are exploring new biological and social space; but we will follow them. They are the one minority group to which all of us, with a little luck, will belong. But instead of observing their explorations with self-interested curiosity, we transfer the exotic nature of the new social territory to the individuals exploring it, and keep our distance.

This psychological feat of making foreign or even taboo something as inevitable as our own aging suggests that old age is the kind of painful topic that most needs the telephoto-focusing of cross-cultural examination. Traditionally, cross-cultural researchers have used enforced distance from the exotic to see some aspect of human life more clearly, then brought that distance back home for a better understanding of the familiar. There is a slight reversal in this process when applied to old age, in itself revealing of our habitual ways of thinking about the elderly. The typical anthropological investigation often began with interest in some apparently bizarre behavior in a distant culture. The gradual understanding of that behavior as reasonable in its context revealed previously invisible links between our own actions and their cultural setting. The reversal in old-age research is that it is certain behaviors of our own old people—age-homogeneous communities, for example—which seem strange but become understandable in the light of cross-cultural examination.

The title of the book comes from the major finding of cross-cultural research so far: old people are people. I am often asked the following rather querulous question: But isn't everything you're saying about old people just like students in dorms, or soldiers in camps, or anyone who's suffered a loss, and so on? Of course it is—which pleases me, but seems to annoy the audience. Our expectation that old people are different is so strong that it is annoying to be told, and difficult to believe, that they behave very much as other human beings under similar conditions and in similar cultural contexts. We don't need special "old-people theory" to understand what old people do and feel. We apparently do need a great deal of evidence to persuade ourselves that old people are people, and to understand how the same cultural compensations or constraints that affect all humans shape what it means to be an old person in various social settings. The goal of this book is a cross-cultural examination of age, which will bring us closer, both theoretically and personally, to understanding old people and old age.

Anthropologists have often worked with the old, but age itself is a new focus for cross-cultural study. Ethnographers visiting traditional societies around the world have spent many hours with old people, who know the customs, remember what the society was like before outside contacts, and perhaps most important, have the time to spend hours talking with a curious anthropologist. Although old people have been important informants, however, the topic of conversation was seldom old age itself. Cross-cultural study of old people, or of age as a factor in social organization, is a recent form of the long-standing alliance between anthropologists and the aged (Keith 1980a).

Understanding old people as people, as human actors in culturally defined settings, requires several perspectives central to anthropological research: cross-cultural comparison, holistic analysis of context, and subjective data. First, a *cross-cultural comparative* approach is necessary to distinguish universal aspects of aging from the diversity of social responses to it. Second, old age must be considered in *context*. The effect of social and cultural context on what it means to be old emerges from the comparisons mentioned above. Another context from which old age must not be isolated is that of the life course. To understand the significance of age as a social identity late in life, it is essential to know what was its importance at other points, such as adolescence. Finally, the meaning of age and its uses in society must be considered from the point of view of the *actors*—that is, of the old people themselves.

These anthropological perspectives provide the central themes of this book. The rest of this chapter outlines the development of cross-cultural research on old age. The following chapters explore the various ways that age assumes social significance—in cognitive categorizations, norms and ideologies, informal interactions, formal groups. Every dimension of age as a social border is examined for its effect on older people. Also, as the boundary image indicates, age as a social phenomenon must be seen from various vantages: that of the individuals in a particular age category as well as of those in whatever other age divisions are recognized in a particular context. Emphasis is on the subjective situation of old people, but that influences, and is influenced by, the perceptions and expectations of others.

The Status and Treatment of Old People

The first and major continuing focus in cross-cultural study of old age is status. Perhaps because early Western researchers were surprised to see old people in positions of power and prestige, they reported those cases prominently and developed theories to explain this exotic behavior. I found, for instance, in a study of sixty traditional (small-scale, non-industrial) societies that explicit statements by ethnographers about age as an important principle in the society were correlated with status differences based on age, but not with other reported uses of age, such as division of labor, differences in dress, or access to food.

The ancestral model for cross-cultural studies of old age is Simmons's 1945 work on *The Role of the Aged in Primitive Society*. Comparing seventy-one societies, Simmons discovered that higher status for old people was derived from traditional skills and knowledge; greater security came from property rights; food from communal sharing and exemptions from taboos; and their general welfare was guaranteed by their families in exchange for routine services such as babysitting, cooking, or mending. A more recent study identified information control as a key factor. Old people around the world have higher status when they control important information. When they consult, make decisions, arbitrate, teach, they get special food privileges, seating arrangements, and verbal deference (Maxwell and Silverman 1970). It has also been speculated that the reason it made evolutionary sense for early human societies to take care of old people was that when the memory was the only available storehouse for information, living a long time made old people precious archives. Societies with such stores of information might therefore have been more successful than those with less longevity (Katz 1978).

"So what else is new?" might be the reaction to this list. Old people are respected when they control information or resources, and when they can offer useful services. My answer to the question is "not much is new." In most parts of the world, and for a long time, the same things have provided prestige for old people as for anyone else. The question is whether old people are excluded from or have special access to those possibilities.

Social change and modernization have been blamed by several scholars as conditions detrimental to the status of old people. The role of old people as living storehouses of information, for example, is less valuable when changes make their knowledge obsolete, or when books and computers can keep more information more efficiently (Maxwell and Silverman 1970). Prestige is often also more available to the young in situations of change, since they then have a chance to acquire skills and resources independently of their elders (Press and McKool 1972). One comparison of fifteen societies showed that, in general, higher levels of modernization are detrimental to the position of the aged (Cowgill and Holmes 1972).

However, this general relationship is now being reconsidered. Fortunately—because otherwise there might be an invidious tendency to believe that a good position for the old is part of a primitive, traditional way of life, and no longer possible in modern society. The

Cross-cultural studies show great variations in the status of old people. On the left, a grandmother grinding corn in a Central Mexican household performs a useful service and encourages respect and reciprocal support for herself. On the right, a beggar in Mexico City suffers the fate of some old people in rapidly modernizing societies. (Photos by Jay Sokolovsky)

evidence does not support this, for several reasons. First, comparison of the position of old people in a wider range of societies shows that although their situation does decline from traditional to modern society, it goes up again in the *most* modern (Cowgill 1974; Palmore and Manton 1974). The relationship between modernization and the status of old people is what scientists call curvilinear: at first more modernization means lower status, but then at a certain point the direction shifts, and with further increasing levels of modernization the old have more status. Sighing about the evils of modernization is therefore no excuse for tolerating a low position for the aged. Second, the old days were not so good. 84 percent of the societies in a world-wide sample treat their elderly in some non-supportive way, ranging from insults to murder (Glascock and Feinman 1981).

A misleading support for the false notion that old people always do well in traditional society and are doomed to difficulties in modern contexts comes from the assumption that the position of the aged in traditional societies is always the same. The studies of status do not show that; they identify conditions under which old people do better, but those conditions do not always apply. There is great variability in the position of old people in traditional societies. Consider, for instance, these old people's complaints: "The concept of family solidarity has been reduced to a meaningless ideal. Old people get respect on ritual occasions, but in everyday life these ideals are ignored. The truly aged retire into insignificance and fade away. Many old people cannot sleep well because of worry and the unsympathetic attitude of their family around them. Old people may be spit at, or even hit." (Harlan 1968, pp. 474–75) Where? In agricultural villages of India. *But* property goes to sons early and political councils are made up of property owners. In short, this is a traditional setting, but the conditions for high status do not apply. Another source of over-rosy views of the traditional situation of old people is failure to distinguish what people practice from what they preach, or their behaviors from their attitudes. The same cultures that permit lack of support for the old, even up to killing them, also prescribe respect and deference (Glascock and Feinman 1980).

Finally, there are indications that change may have positive consequences for old people, depending on what kind of change it is. Among the Coast Salish Indians, for example, a religious revival has brought prestige and power to the old people, the only ones who will remember the dances and songs needed for traditional religious rituals (Amoss 1981). It is possible that revivals of any kind may improve the prestige of the old, at least temporarily. The *Foxfire* phenomenon may be another example of cultural revival beneficial to the elderly. These reports by Appalachian high school students of encounters with old people and their crafts are a commercial publishing success, and seem likely to raise levels of concern and respect for the elderly.

Pension programs have also made old people valuable—in a literal sense—and therefore desirable members of households in the USSR, and in the United States during the Depression. These are examples of a change in the political and economic circumstances making sources of higher status more available to the elderly. These types of programs are one reason why the change-status relationship is curvilinear—i.e., that the position of the old improves in the most modern societies.

One last important reminder about old people and change is that the old are not always the dependent variable, are not always on the effect side of the equation: they are also causes of change. It is still another indication of the ways we are accustomed to thinking about old people that we have virtually assumed that what needed to be studied was how various changes affected them. They are also actors, and the actions that old people in industrial societies take now will have a profound influence on the roles of old people in the future. Because it is a new phenomenon in the history of humanity for a large proportion of a population to enjoy a long period of life in old age, the meaning of that new life stage is not yet defined. The role models for that life stage are the old-age pioneers who are exploring it now, and their experiments in community formation, or political organization, are active sources of social change.

Culture and Personality

Culture is "the design for living" passed down the generations in every human group. A second major focus in cross-cultural research on old age is the effect of culture on the elderly. What is the influence of deeply rooted cultural values on the experience of being old in various settings? One answer is that they may drive you crazy. In the United States, for example, two anthropologists discovered through comparisons of mentally healthy and mentally ill old people that the individuals who had the strongest attachments to core American values such as independence and aggressiveness were the most likely to be mentally ill. In other words, the old people who clung to the values shared by younger Americans were in psychic trouble, confronted with the impossibility of realizing those ideals (Clark and Anderson 1967).

Cat food vs. dependence is not a universal dilemma for the old. In many societies, dependence on others is not feared, so that old people requiring support are not forced to renounce a precious value in exchange for adequate food, shelter, or health care. Interdependence, or reciprocity, would be better labels than dependence for perceptions of support for old people in Japan or Mexico. Two differences in the ways members of different cultural communities perceive social relations may have great influence on attitudes toward support for older people. Awareness of interdependence is one. Members of most human communities are highly interdependent, although the degree to which that interdependence is personalized, and consequently highly visible and salient, varies widely. In modern industrial societies, our extreme dependence on others derives from the high degree of specialization. However, the impersonality and segmentation of much of our lives may mask that interdependence during most of our adult years, leaving us open to great psychic stress if old age brings a more personalized, visible, and therefore unacceptable need for support from others (Clark 1972). A second cultural influence on attitudes about care for the aged is more temporal. The time depth used may be the difference between interpretation of care as reciprocity or dependence. "I have nothing to give in return" is often the great concern of American older people in need of help, especially from children. To people in many societies, this would seem a remarkably shortsighted view of the life course. If the entire life is used as a balance sheet, as is the case in many views of the world, then care for old people is more likely to be seen as reciprocity than as dependence.

Although—not surprisingly—no society seems to place a positive value on the physical aging process per se, different "designs for living" offer more or less social and psychic compensation for the pains of physical age. Using psychological tests, Gutmann has discovered what he interprets as universal shifts in orientation to the world from active to passive to magical mastery (1968; 1974). As the men he interviewed in Kansas City, on the Golan Heights, in Yucatan, and in Navaholand grow older, they shift from attempts to control the external world (active) to a greater tendency to accommodate to it (passive), to denials of unpleasant reality and a focus on other spheres of reality, such as the supernatural (magical). Although as Clark and Anderson (1967) point out, such a sequence may make old people "un-American," other cultures, such as that of the Druze in Israel and Lebanon, offer old men a socially valued position in ritual roles congruent to their personality shifts.

What compensations a cultural system may guarantee to all old people must be distinguished from those available only to some. Old women are allowed by many cultures to loosen their tongues, both in vulgar speech and in political councils (e.g., Simmons 1945, pp. 64–65; Middleton 1966). Old age also guarantees ritual authority to old men in African societies such as Samburu or Tallensi. Among the Tiwi of Australia, by contrast, old men have only a headstart on the accumulation of the many wives that are the source of wealth and prestige. It is almost impossible for a young Tiwi to achieve highest status in the community, but not all old men achieve it either. Some use their age advantage more shrewdly than others. Eskimo elderly have a handicap rather than an advantage in their race for status and social participation. The best their culture offers them are strategies for staying in the running, either by delaying the worst consequences of old age or by renewing certain youthful roles. Older men, for instance, hunt at the beginnings and endings of a season to avoid competition; women attempt to adopt children after they can no longer bear their own (Guemple 1969). For these Eskimo old people, shrewdness is needed to minimize their handicap rather than to capitalize on an advantage; they have in common with the Tiwi that neither success nor failure is guaranteed to all old people on the basis of age in either society.

Community Studies

The attempt to understand a world of older people in its own terms is highly consistent with the approach anthropologists have taken in other unknown territories, but is in sharp contrast to much research on old people. Most studies have asked questions about old people and their families, or old people as subjects of social policy, or old people in relation to younger generations. Our questions have been mainly about old people and *us*. Research in communities of

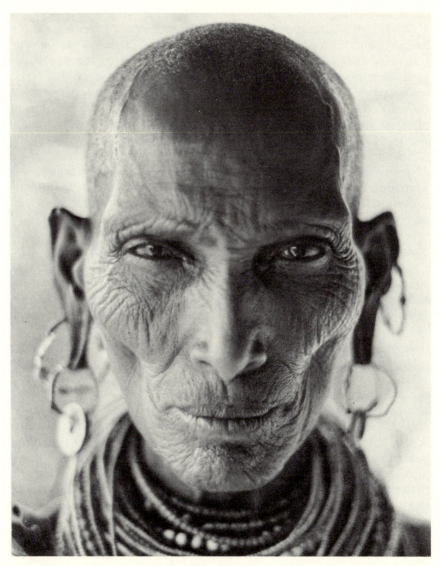

Women past child-bearing age become freer and more influential in many cultures (Rendille Tribe, Kenya). (Photo by Asmarom Legesse)

old people shifts the center of inquiry to their relations among themselves, and to their ways of dealing with the outside world.

Community is an old focus for comparative study, but the newest one in cross-cultural research with the aged. Since the late 1960s, several anthropologists have given old people their classic treatment for little known social groups: they have moved in on them and observed their daily lives. In public housing in England and the United States, union residences in France, and American church homes, condominiums, and mobile home parks with assorted ethnic and social class life-styles, ethnographers have studied the new social worlds created by older people living among themselves.

The first finding about old people in separate residences is that they do create communities. New social worlds emerge in the new physical spaces. Once again, "the old people are people" theme recurs, as the factors that promote community creation among the old are the same ones that have operated in the histories of a great diversity of communities: among urban squatters, utopian experimenters, nation states. As in those cases, the old people in many different kinds of housing have been stimulated to form bonds of community by such factors as lack of alternative, high levels of investment, external threat, communal work, and participation in collective events (Keith 1980b).

The communities formed by old people have many things in common with each other; the first is that there is much they do *not* share with the social contexts in which they are embedded. Distinctiveness from the outside is visible in various ways, which are discussed in detail in chapter 5. Social identities derived from past lives take on new meanings: in the French residence I studied, making Christmas decorations is a Communist activity. Mardi Gras has become a Communist celebration, and only non-Communists attend the pottery club (Ross 1977). Identities highly salient outside may also become less relevant than common age. In public housing in the United States, where several ethnic groups are mixed, relations across ethnic lines are more harmonious than in the cities outside. Sex roles within the communities are often different from those outside it. Men and women may become more alike as social actors than they were previously, or new kinds of activities may become the markers of sex distinctions. Status is not assigned in external terms. Although there are status rankings, they are emphatically not in terms of past achievement or based on the usual outside sources such as occupation, income, or age itself. These are usually quite rigorously made irrelevant, and prestige is assigned on internal grounds such as leadership in community activities, personal popularity, or skill at leisure pursuits. Among themselves, old people also define distinctive norms about death and sex. There are powerful bonds of social support within these communities. Both material and emotional resources are shared, and the recognition of these ties is expressed in references to "our community," "we residents," and "we old people."

Participation in community seems to have the same benefits for old people as for other people. Comparative studies of similar old people who have moved into mixed-age versus separate age settings suggest that those living with other old people have higher morale (Bultena 1974; Teaff, Lawton, and Carlson 1977). It may be that the benefits of community are magnified for the old, who are often excluded from active participation in mixed-age communities, or left stranded when the community moves away.

Clearly, what is intriguing in the study of old-age communities is not how different the old people are, but once again, how much they act like everyone else given the opportunity. A cross-cultural perspective which expands that "everyone else" category to include age groups in traditional societies may explain both *why* age has emerged as a basis of community among the old and *how* age groups may provide that opportunity to "act like everyone else."

There are, first of all, separate age villages or sections of villages in several African societies, and my comparisons of a worldwide sample of traditional societies show that spatial separation of age groups at some point in the life course is very common. This residential feature of age groups in industrial and traditional societies is only their most superficial parallel. More profound similarities are their egalitarian values, the balancing of kin ties with age-group loyalties, distinctive norms and rituals, mutual aid among age-mates, opposition to other ages, and socialization by peers into age-appropriate norms and behaviors.

The cross-cultural comparisons of age groups presented in later chapters suggest some explanations for why old people in the United States group together even in the face of reactions from younger individuals who brand it a depressing segregation. As if they had read the reports from Africa or Latin America, some old people are creating age bonds that offer them support for satisfying lives not provided by their modern societies. Egalitarianism insulates them from an outside status system in which they have a low position, made more painful by the fact that they may have sunk there for the first time in their adult lives. Mutual aid among age-mates provides both material and psychic security without the high price of dependence. Instead of being norm maintainers, as in traditional societies, the concern of modern old people with norms is creative: they invent responses to sex, death, conflict, or economic need that are distinctive to their new communities. The norms they define and the rites of passage into these new social systems ease the pain of social ambiguity—the literally inhuman situation in which many old people otherwise exist. As a community of age peers, old people are less dependent on their families for all social satisfactions and consequently often enjoy better relations with kin. Age groups may also ritualize intergenerational conflicts on a formal, collective level and relieve strain in specific individual relationships.

These cross-cultural similarities suggest, first of all, that what is often seen as odd or controversial behavior by old people in industrial societies is perhaps a reasonable and functional adaptation to the situation in which they find themselves. Our reluctance to accept that is related not only to American attitudes toward old age, and our tendency to think of old people as different than the rest of us, but also to our discomfort with *explicit* emphasis on social differentiation of any kind.

Age Differentiation

Placed in a comparative perspective, the ethnographic studies of old people's communities lead to the broader questions of age differentiation. As soon as old people as age-mates are considered along with individuals of other ages and in other cultures who group together by age, we are faced with basic questions about the *conditions* under which age becomes a significant social border, and the *consequences* of various types and levels of age differentiation for both individuals and societies. This kind of broad question about age in social organization is an important step toward integration of old people into cross-cultural theories of human behavior.

Integration versus segregation of the elderly has been a major theme in gerontology (see Rosow 1967, 1974; Carp 1976). As scholars, however, we have been rather like the racial integrationists who want to move an ethnic minority into someone else's neighborhood. We have not really integrated old people into our own theories, but accumulating evidence that "old people are people" is bringing us to the point of practicing as well as preaching integration. Age differentiation provides a guide to understanding the perceptions, feelings, and actions of old people in the same terms as those of individuals at any age.

Age differentiation is the framework for the rest of this book. Each chapter will concentrate on one dimension of age differentiation—cognitive, ideological, normative, social, or corporate. Analysis of examples of age borders in a wide range of cultural contexts will suggest the conditions that promote various kinds of significance for age. Finally, we will ask the "so what" question about consequences of these different uses of age for old people.

Dimensions of Age Differentiation

Social boundaries based on any characteristic may have one or more dimensions: cognitive, ideological, normative, social, or corporate (Ross 1975). In terms of any dimension, a characteristic may be the basis for various numbers of borders, and each boundary may be higher or lower—that is, defined with varying degrees of sharpness. By definition, any border has two sides, so perceptions and evaluations may be different for insiders and outsiders. Symbolic markers of a social border must also be distinguished from the basis of the boundary itself; i.e., age may be the characteristic grouping individuals together, but the indicator of that common characteristic could be different from the points of view of different individuals, or in different cultural contexts, or at different points in time. The boundary uses of a characteristic must also be mapped on social, individual, and situational levels. There may be historical or economic factors that promote generational conflict in a society, for instance. There will be individual variation, however, in orientation toward other age groups and the salience of age. In addition, situational features such as age composition of a conversational group or the topic of discussion may also affect both attitudes and actions related to age

The Cognitive Dimension

The cognitive dimension of age as a social boundary refers to its use as a principle of categorization. Do people use age to categorize individuals? How many categories do they identify? What are the reasons for different age categorizations in different societies, or for different individuals at different times? What difference does it make to old people whether many distinctions are made on the basis of age or only a few broad categories? What are the consequences of asymmetry in evaluation of either the old-age border or its symbolic markers by younger and older?

The Normative-Ideological Dimension

Individuals who recognize that they share some characteristic, or who realize that others perceive them as sharing it, may develop a sense of collectivity or shared fate, norms about how they should behave, and beliefs about how others should treat them. In terms of age, the question is what conditions will stimulate ideological responses to age? If age ideologies are available, what will lead some individuals to subscribe to them, others not? When age-mates develop shared norms, what will their content be: under what conditions are norms most likely to be distinctive, rather than reflections of those for other ages? What are the degrees of differences in norms about age-appropriate behavior held by individuals of different ages? What situational variation is there in the appeal of age ideology, or in the force of norms? What are the consequences for older people of the existence of age ideologies, or of the development of distinctive norms among age-mates?

The Interactional Dimension

Individuals who share what they or others perceive as the "same" age may or may not concentrate their social activity inside the social border that age defines. Deciding on the extent to which they do this requires more than counting hours or individuals. The significant calculation for charting an interactional dimension is what proportion of *kinds* of social contact people share predominantly with age-mates. For each kind of social tie, such as friendship, a person may have a more or less age-homogeneous repertory of others; and out of the entire range of types of social links, a greater or smaller proportion may be predominantly age-homogeneous. We need to discover when age-mates are most likely to provide a major part of social support for each other. Are there certain points in the life course when peer ties are particularly important, such as adolescence and old age? Is this true universally, and if so, why? Are there certain social situations when peers are most likely to stick together? Do various types of society promote age bonds more than others? What are the effects on old people of having an important proportion of age-mates in their social networks?

The Corporate Dimension

An age border may also be formalized as the principle of re-cruitment into a corporate group. The groups that indicate age differentiation on a corporate dimension have an explicit focus on age. There are age-homogeneous groups with other manifest pur-poses, but they do not represent this explicit corporate dimension. These groups are not only recruited by age, but age is also central to their corporate operation. Since the goals of age organizations are diverse, we need to discover not only what conditions promote organization around age, but also what factors lead to various goals for that association. Organization as a social fact must also be distin-guished from any particular individual's decision to participate. From the point of view of consequences for old people, we must ask both what are the effects of the existence of old-age associations (even on old people who never join), and what are the effects of membership in various types?

The plan of this book corresponds to a map of age differentia-tion. By charting the conditions and consequences of different levels and degrees of age differentiation on each dimension, its goal is to reintegrate questions about the meaning of age for American old people into a broader view of the human life course in cross-cultural perspective.

Chapter

2

Thinking About Age: The Cognitive Dimension

Age-Grades, Age-Sets, and Age-Groups

Use of age as a basis of social categorization ranges from the minimal distinction of young, adult, and old through the complexities of systems with six or more named "grades" sliced through the life course, or even two systems—one based on age, one on generation. Among the St. Lawrence Island Eskimo, age is used simply to separate boys from men, girls from women; men and women as they mature "continue doing what (they have) always done as long as possible," then finally enter old age (Hughes 1961). Toward the opposite extreme of age differentiation are the Arusha of Kenya. Members of this agricultural tribe recognize six formal age statuses or *grades:* youths, junior warriors, senior warriors, junior elders, senior elders, and retired elders. Approximately every five years, an *age-set* is created, including all the young men circumcised together in initiation ceremonies during that period. Age-set membership crosscuts all of Arusha society, but the entire set seldom acts together, and then only on internal business or ritual of the age organization. Local *age-groups* of men initiated together in one neighborhood do form a corporate entity. Public rites of passage move members of an age-set through the progression of age-grades.

The distinctions between age-grades, sets, and groups are parallel to the differences between the American concepts of senior year in high school (grade), the graduation class of a particular year (set), and the individuals who were seniors together in a particular high school in a given year (group) (see Radcliffe-Brown 1929, and Gulliver

1968 for discussion of terminology). In this chapter on cognitive maps of the life course, our focus is on the grades or statuses.

There is wide cross-cultural variation in the number of age grades or statuses that divide the life course. In a comparative study of sixty traditional societies, I found a range from two to eight for both men and women. The most common number of grades for men is five, for women, two. Most specific examples of age-set activities in the anthropological literature refer to men. It is still not clear from the evidence we have whether most age-set organizations are male, or whether most age-set organizations *about which we have information* are male (Kertzer and Madison 1981). Certainly most of the age-sets described in anthropological books and articles are male, although there are a few female examples in East and West Africa and Brazil (Gessain 1971; Ottenberg 1971; Maybury-Lewis forthcoming). In my quantitative cross-cultural study, almost a third of the sixty sample societies had male age-sets, just over 10 percent had age-sets for women. In the few cases that have been reported, the women's sets seem to have less social significance and to share fewer and less elaborate rituals. They are sometimes described as more like "ladies auxiliaries" to the male organizations than distinct women's systems.

There have been interesting speculations about the apparent absence of women's age organization in most societies. Women are more tightly integrated into familial roles than men, and these kinship ties may stress vertical family bonds to the exclusion of the horizontal bonds of age (Gulliver 1968; Kertzer and Madison 1981). If age ties are seen as a balance to kin bonds (discussed below), then women who stay within the domestic sphere would be less likely to participate in formal age-groups than men whose lives are to a great extent played out in public spheres where principles other than kinship also operate. Men's age-groups have also been interpreted as related to the transition young men must make from the domestic sphere to the public. Most women do not have to weather this discontinuity (Eisenstadt 1956; Whiting, Kluckhohn, and Anthony 1958; Young and Bacdayan 1962).

Some support for this comes from the Ibo of Nigeria, where women are organized into age-groups which play an important role in women's trade businesses in the public market (Ottenberg 1971). Ibo women's age-sets have also become more significant since pre-colonial times, as women have acquired more independence from the home. The tendency for the male-female distinction to take priority over any age differences among women may also be particularly strong in patrilocal communities where a woman's move into her husband's territory places her with many other unrelated women among a network of male kin (Kertzer and Madison 1981).

Age-sets may also be predominantly male because men need

them more. Since transitions in the female life course are more neatly marked by nature on an individual basis, age-setting could also be seen as a cultural compensation for men.

Finally, the tentative "ifs" and "mays" of this discussion point toward speculation that the apparent absence of women's age organization may derive from lack of research. Like many other aspects of women's lives, women's age-sets may not have been reported because male ethnographers did not—or could not—learn about them. The two most clearly documented cases of women's age-sets are in fact described by women anthropologists (Gessain 1971; Ottenberg 1971; pointed out in Kertzer and Madison 1981). A general cause of lack of information about women's lives is the tendency of researchers to concentrate on the more public and formalized aspects of culture in which men are the stars. Recent increased attention to more informal and intimate aspects of various cultures has been stimulated by women's studies, and should reveal much about less formal and more subtle significance of age for both men and women.

Marking Age Borders

Chronological and Functional Definitions

In many societies, when people can no longer work, they are defined as old; in our own, the situation is reversed—when people are defined as old, they can no longer work. The distinction is between two ways of marking an age border. One is functional, in terms of what people can do; the other is chronological, based on the number of years they have lived. Although functional definitions are the most common worldwide, there is not a neat split between traditional and modern societies corresponding to use of functional versus chronological age. The pastoral Fulani of West Africa, for example, keep close track of their chronological ages, while half the Americans in a recent national survey did *not* use a number of years to answer the question "At what age does the average man or woman become old?" (NCOA 1976, pp. 22–25). Even in traditional societies where age is not reckoned in calendar years, there may be some arbitrary means of determining when individuals move from one age category to another. Among the Nandi of Kenya, for instance, the signal for age-grade transitions is the flowering of the *setiot* bush. The essential similarity to calendar counting is, of course, that the functional abilities of the individual are not the basis for age categorization, which leaves open the possibility that the two may not be congruent.

The most common definition of old age in a recent comparative study of sixty traditional societies was a shift in social role, such as change in work responsibility or the adult status of children (Glascock and Feinman 1980, 1981). The next most common was chronological years; the least used was a change in physical capability, such as senility or invalidism. These researchers, after careful reading of the ethnographic reports, feel that the emphasis on chronology is misleading. Because it rarely occurs alone, but usually along with one of the other definitions, they are suspicious that chronological definition of age is imposed by Western anthropologists who estimate in years the timing of age transitions defined by their informants in terms of social role. We may even do this at home: Americans who define old age in years also typically refer to the reasons people are old at that point, such as retirement, physical decline, or change in mental attitude (NCOA 1976, pp. 22–23).

The rare occurrence of physical capability as a marker of old age in the cross-cultural sample may result from most people being classified as old *before* they become physically impaired. Support for this notion would come from evidence that many societies distinguish two categories of old, those still active, and those who are decrepit. This is precisely what the cross-cultural data show. One-third of the sixty representative societies make distinctions among different groups of old people, and over one-fourth explicitly divide the old into young-old and old-old. Phrases such as "overaged," "sleeping period," or "already dead" are used for the final declining stage.

"What's in a name?" In the case of old age, it may be a matter of life or death. Societies in which old people are killed or abandoned all make this intact-decrepit or young-old–old-old distinction. This is perhaps the appropriate place for a word about the Eskimos and the ice floes. Abandonment of old people to float away on ice floes is often used as the ultimate example of bad treatment for the elderly. Although it is a stretch in nonethnocentric thought to imagine otherwise, there is in fact a correlation between killing old people and their high status and good treatment. In many societies where old people are sometimes killed or abandoned, they are well treated and respected until they become very feeble, when the killing or abandonment is done often at their request, and by a very close relative. The behaviors are not inconsistent if we remember the two categories of old people: the intact or young-old are supported by the society as long as they can participate, and finally hurried toward death when they enter the decrepit or old-old phase. Killing or abandonment of old people is rare around the world (19 percent of the sixty-society sample), and from the comparative study appears to occur in societies where equality is highly valued and in which the resources are scarce (Glascock and Feinman 1980, 1981).

Chronological versus functional definition of age was identified as a factor in attitudes toward old people in one comparative study of Quechua Indians, Greenland Eskimos, Japanese, Burmese, and north Indians. The accurate measurement of time, and the calculation of the point at which people should retire and should die may make people anxious about aging. When function rather than chronology is the indicator of old age, there is also the possibility of a more gradual transition to being old. The same American survey referred to above offers some confirmation. Those Americans who feel that people over sixty-five are very useful members of their community are less likely to define old age in number of years than those who feel that people over sixty-five are not very useful members of their community (NCOA 1976 p. 24).

Functionality itself has different meanings, and therefore must be measured differently in different cultural contexts. Depending on what is required for full social participation in various settings, and on the availability and cultural interpretation of social and physical supports, individuals with similar physical capabilities may be more or less able to function in different communities. If part of being a functional adult is maintenance of an independent household, and part of maintaining an independent household is carrying water from a well a mile away, even a relatively healthy old person might not function adequately. If, however, the usual household organization provides a grandchild to carry the water, the same individual may be "intact" or functional far longer.

Standardized indicators of functionality are widely used in the United States. Old people are asked if they can climb stairs, take a bath, clip their toenails. Such measures are of course no more universally applicable than the distance to water. The title of a widely used scale for measuring functionality in old age makes the point explicit: "Activities of Daily Living." If ability to carry out the "Activities of Daily Living" is a reasonable measure of functionality, then functionality cannot be measured in a particular context until we know what people have to do there to get through a day. A necessary preliminary step in research on functionality must be discovery of its measures, which requires the patient watching and listening of the technique anthropologists call *participant observation* (Keith 1980c). A major challenge to comparative research—including that across ethnic and class boundaries within modern societies—is the discovery of adequate measures for functionality (Eckert and Beall 1980).

Physical anthropologists have very recently begun to take up this challenge, extending their previous interest in comparative study of human physical development beyond adulthood into old age. As

When age is calculated by ability rather than by chronology, a vigorous old person can remain an active community member regardless of years. (Photo by Jay Sokolovsky)

they have already done for child-to-adult development, these re-searchers are now trying to discover relationships among biological age (e.g., skeletal or dental development), chronological age, and functionality for older adults in various cultures. One physical an-thropologist, for example, goes to the high Himalayas to observe the aging process among Sherpa. She asks her somewhat puzzled infor-mants to empty their lungs into balloons, grip strength meters, and have their blood pressure taken to provide baseline physical informa-tion. She also observes their participation in community life, and estimates age when necessary by connecting births with events such as eclipses or wars. Sherpa old in years do not suffer from many ills Americans think of as inevitable aspects of aging. However, many Sherpa are dissatisfied with their community participation because they feel dependent if they share a home with any child except the youngest son, who is often away working (Beall forthcoming; see also Van Arsdale 1980 and Howell 1974, 1976, and 1979).

Physical Age and Social Age

"You old witch" is an epithet thought, if not actually hurled, by young people resentful of a powerful elder in many societies, including those not officially supposed to believe in witchcraft. The directions in which such insults are aimed can be revealing indicators of the cleavages of stress and conflict.

A naturalistic experiment conducted in the Sudan used witchcraft accusations as evidence for intergenerational tensions, and concluded that wide discrepancy between age categorization and individual functional ability leads to conflict across age lines (Nadel 1952). The Korongo and the Mesakin provide a naturalistic experiment because they are extremely similar in many ways but differ in their age categorization and intergenerational relations. Since so many other features of the societies are "controlled for," the differences in relations between age-groups can plausibly be accounted for by the differences in age categorization.

Among the Korongo, there is no belief in witchcraft; the Mesakin, their close neighbors, with the same economy, political system, religion, and kinship organization and household structure, are "literally obsessed" by fear of witchcraft. Although the fear is general, the sources and objects of witchcraft are very specific. An older man is always the alleged witch, accused of attempting to harm a younger man. The Mesakin explain this by what they assume are older men's resentments of the young. The most common pair in witchcraft struggles is the mother's brother and sister's son. In this society, the nephew inherits from his uncle and is entitled to an anticipatory inheritance which the uncle must give him on demand. It is the quarrel over this required gift that triggers most witchcraft conflicts.

The reason that "old men" in Mesakin may be resentful of the young is that they are not chronologically old. There are only three age-grades, and men enter the oldest one in their late twenties. In addition, the change in expected behavior when a new grade is entered is very abrupt. Men must give up the privileges of youthful masculine vigor—wrestling, spear-fighting, and living in cattle camps—abruptly and absolutely while they are physically very young. The Korongo, virtually a twin society in every other respect, have twice as many age categories on their social map of the life course. Social age is far more congruent with physical and, in addition, the transitions in expected behavior are more gradual (Nadel 1952).

Exotic details of spears or cattle herding should not obscure the similarities to the situation of older people in our society. The two key factors producing intergenerational conflict among Mesakin seem to be the incongruity between physical and social age and the abruptness with which men are supposed to make the behavioral changes appropriate to the new grade. Both of these have been present in American mandatory retirement systems: many individuals are physically far more youthful at sixty-five than mandatory retirement rules imply. For most people, also, the shift from employment to retirement is abrupt. The lack of clear definition for the role of retirement might be seen as better or worse than the Mesakin situation, in which, although it is undesirable, at least there is a definition.

Advancing mandatory retirement to seventy in the United States provides more congruity between physical and social age; the Mesakin example suggests that this may reduce intergenerational tensions. Abruptness of role shift may still be present, however, and if the roles are undesirable or unclear, tension may still be promoted. If mandatory retirement based on age is abolished altogether, the congruity between social and physical age could be complete. Two categories might emerge—retired person and old person—with functional rather than chronological bases. The Mesakin hypotheses predict that such a situation would reduce tensions between younger and older. As we will see in discussion of transition rituals, however, other factors may intrude—for example, indeterminate age-grade transitions may stimulate more conflict than fixed timing.

Individual Perceptions of Age Categories

Since the cognitive dimension of age differentiation refers to age as a basis for sorting individuals into categories, one anthropologist used a card-sorting research strategy to discover people's perceptions of social age (Fry 1976). Adults in a United States city were given thirty-four cards describing hypothetical persons in terms of their career stage, educational level, and domestic situation, including marital status, children's marital and parental status, and household composition: "a female, high school graduate, single, working, living with parents"; or "a male, widowed, retired, living with adult children." They were asked first to sort out the cards in terms of appropriate age or similarity in age bracket, then to assign rough chronological ages to the piles, then to label them with words, and finally to identify themselves with one of the age-groups they had defined.

The results are, first of all, a warning about how cautiously to view discussions (such as ours above) which generalize about age categorization on a social level. The reason for caution is that these Americans did not agree in their categorizations. Some identified as many as fifteen different age-grades, others as few as two, and there were over two hundred different labels for categories. It is certainly likely that there is less individual variation in some traditional societies than in the culturally diverse United States. Since generalizations about age categorizations in traditional societies are seldom based on the kind of careful sampling of the population that this study represents, however, what variation there is is probably obscured.

There were patterns in the ways the Americans categorized the cards that seem to explain why they had varying views of age. The numbers of age categories identified is higher for people who are married than for those who are single, divorced, or widowed. Parents with children in their late teens make the fewest age distinctions, and there is a marked increase among parents whose children are moving into adulthood themselves. People make the fewest age categorizations when they themselves are between forty-six and sixty-five, more when they are either younger or older.

Fry suggests that the respondent's stage in the domestic cycle is the reason for the differences in age categorization. She argues that people make more age distinctions when there are individuals of more different ages in their immediate kinship network, i.e., when they have children of their own at home, or when they become grandparents. The middle years, when adult children are leaving home but have not yet started families of their own, is the time when age differences are least significant.

The basic premise linking age categories and individual kin networks is that people make more cognitive distinctions in domains of life where they use those distinctions in action. In other words, Americans don't seem to carry around empty age categories in their heads, but contract their cognitive map to fit the actual territory of their lives. That territory includes more than kinship, and Fry's interpretation could possibly be broadened to include other areas of social life. Age may become less salient as a basis for categorization at points in the life course when more competing principles are available. This would also be in the middle adult years, when occupational and other social roles are the most numerous. In addition, important ties to others the *same* age might make age very salient, as individuals perceive strong similarities to age peers and sharp differences from others. Certain points in the life course, such as the transitions in and out of social maturity around adolescence and retirement, may stimulate this heightened sensitivity to age boundaries, along with more age-homogeneous networks. Age categorization should, then, be more significant before and after the middle years of most intense work, childrearing, and community activity—exactly what Fry found.

The real-life sorting task represented by cognitive categories is also performed in terms of specific individuals. Both others and oneself are assigned to age categories. Not everyone makes these age-grade assignments at the same number of years, and self-evaluations don't always agree with those made by others. Several patterns in age-identification can be discerned on this individual level. The most striking fact about identifying oneself as old in America is that many people do not do it at all, or wait as long as possible before using the label on themselves. When asked what age category they belong in, most Americans over sixty-five say middle-aged. Women delay putting themselves in the old category longer than men; middle class Americans put it off longer than those in other classes.

Certain experiences also make people more likely to see themselves as old. Role losses, such as the death of a spouse or retirement from work, are a cue to many people that they are old: after all, these are things that happen to old people. It is significant that these are social, not physical experiences; people are probably not so much feeling old, as they are acknowledging the expectation that these are experiences of old people.

The class difference in identifying oneself as old might be interpreted in either physical or social terms. Do individuals with harder working lives actually feel older sooner? Or is the acceptance of an age categorization that brings lower status in American society more difficult and more resisted by those whose higher status gives them more to lose? Black scholars have made a similar argument about their observation that black old people have a less difficult adjustment to both social and physical pains of aging in the United States: the black old person experiences these difficulties as less of a contrast with preceding years than the white person with a more privileged past. (On ethnicity and aging, see Trela and Sokolovsky 1979; Gelfand 1982; and Cool 1980.)

A cross-cultural contrast in the kinds of social categorization experienced throughout the life course also suggests very basic differences in what it means to be placed in an old age category in various societies. There are two profoundly different types of social classification: one is based on *ascribed* characteristics, such as race, kinship, or age, which are acquired at birth and not easily manipulated by an individual; the other is based on *achieved* characteristics, which depend at least to some extent on what an individual does in life, such as occupation or education. Some societies are organized primarily in terms of one or the other of these types of classification. Since age is an ascriptive criterion, in societies where categories are mainly achieved, an individual assigned an old age identity experiences a rather shocking shift in *type* of classification. For an individual whose culture uses mainly ascriptive criteria throughout the life course, old age may be a new category, but it does not represent a shift in type of classification. The reason that shift may be described as shocking is that the two categories confront the individual with very different possibilities. Ascriptive identities are perceived as unchangeable; achieved identities by definition are supposed to be to some extent controlled by the individual. A person who has felt and valued control over his or her social identity throughout adult life may indeed be shocked by assignment to a category in which an uncontrollable physical characteristic takes priority over individual attributes or actions. The ascriptive-achieved contrast also offers further insight into differences in response to old age categorization by individuals such as black Americans or women who have lifelong experience with the priority of an ascriptive characteristic (Cool 1981).

Because we are accustomed to thinking of achievement as a preferable mode of social classification to ascription, and of old age as a negative status, it is easy to forget that in some settings an ascribed age status is a source of benefits to the old. In a gerontocratic society such as Samburu, *all* members of the elder age-grade have some authority based on ritual, although there is variation among elders in the amount of power and respect they acquire (Spencer 1965). Old age may also be an advantage in the achievement game. Among the Tiwi of Australia, for instance, high status is not assigned to all the old, but it is impossible for a young man to acquire the many women who provide the many work hours needed to achieve the wealth and influence that produce high position (Hart and Pilling 1960).

Individuals in America who identify themselves as old seem to feel both better and worse: worse than those of younger ages, and than themselves in the past; better than others of their own age. They are, in addition, more likely to try to do something about what they perceive as the bad aspects of being old. In a national attitude survey taken in the 1970s, for instance, the people over sixty who identified themselves as "old" were less optimistic about their financial situation, and more likely to support greater federal action in providing medical care and controlling inflation (Bengtson and Cutler 1976, p. 154).

What might be called the "silver-lining effect" of identifying oneself as old is that most individuals who do so then perceive themselves as better off than others in that age category. The mechanism is what sociologists called the *reference group,* and its operation reveals a rather ironically positive consequence of American negative perceptions of old age. An individual's reference group is the category of others to whom he or she refers for evaluation, either by asking "what would they think?" or "how am I doing compared to them?" When a person accepts categorization as old, then other old people become a reference group. (Under certain conditions agemates also become a source of norms, which will be discussed in Chapter 3.) For example, when a representative sample of old people in Iowa were asked to talk about their own life situations, *comparative* judgments of their lives with what they assumed to be the situation of other old people explained more about their satisfaction with their own lives than the objective facts about every domain except health (Bultena and Powers 1976).

The force of comparative judgments is further reinforced by the results of a recent national survey in which Americans of all ages were asked questions about old age. Younger people consistently think that old people are worse off than they are: sicker, poorer, more passive, lonelier (NCOA 1976). Old people also think more highly of themselves than they do of old people on the whole. The old, in other words, share many stereotypes of old age, and feel good as individuals because they don't fit them.

Situational Variation in Age Categorization

It may at first seem contradictory to talk about situational variation of an ascriptive characteristic. The concept of situational ethnicity, introduced by anthropologists working in African cities, is, however, a model for questions about possible contextual variations in the definition or salience of age. It was observed in Africa that ethnic groups which were separate tribes in the country were grouped together as one new "tribe" in the city—at first by others, but eventually by the people themselves (Southall 1970). In addition to this kind of situational differences in definition of ethnicity, there are also variations in its significance. African miners, for instance, grouped together across many ethnic lines in unions opposed to the white owners; in elections for office within the union, however, the competition became tribal (Epstein 1958).

Gerontologists writing about age-grades in American society have pointed to variation in the definition of grades such as "adult" in different institutions or domains (Neugarten and Peterson 1957; Neugarten and Hagestad 1976). The ages at which adulthood is recognized for voting, drinking, driving, and marriage are not congruent in most states. An individual may be grown up in one social domain, but not in others. There are also certain social roles associated with being adult: early work, marriage, parenthood, or independent residence speed up recognition of social maturity; prolonged student status slows it down. This variability is a sharp contrast to some more consistently age-graded societies, in which in any situation in any part of the country it is clear who is junior, who is senior, who is equal. A Nuer man in the Sudan, for example, "has a known age-relationship to every other man in Nuerland with whom he is likely to come into contact, their social attitude to him and his social attitude to them is determined in advance . . ." (Evans-Pritchard 1940; rpt. 1968, p. 258). Even in societies with highly consistent age-grading, there is always one potential source of inconsistency—that between social and genealogical generation. Uncles may be younger than nephews, in other words, or cousins older than parents. Some societies have built-in resolutions to those contradictions with rules assigning priority to one kind of seniority or the other (Needham 1974). In others, the determination is situational.

In addition to this kind of variation, there is also a more unstable kind of situational variation within a society. In another parallel to earlier studies of ethnicity, it has been suggested that in new social situations individuals are likely to give more significance to age as a way of differentiating others (Hess 1972). A similar observation was made about the salience of ethnicity in African cities, where observers suggested that in those confusing new and heterogeneous situations people needed ways of ordering the social world, and ethnicity was a convenient and universally available criterion. The logic should apply to any visible ascriptive characteristic, such as age, and further suggests that as the situation becomes more familiar and individuals more distinguishable, the salience of ethnicity, age, or sex should diminish.

One major exception to this pattern should be new social aggregates where people are all of very similar ages. In fact, retirement communities and public housing for old people offer examples of this kind of situation. The evidence is that within them age becomes less relevant as a way of differentiating individuals (Ross 1977, Chapter 4). When seniority distinctions are made, they are not usually in terms of years but of length of residence (Friedman 1967).

The most powerful consequence of variation in definition or salience of age categories is the possibility it offers for individuals to make choices. If adulthood is defined differently in different domains, an individual can to some extent choose to be more or less adult. Planners facing decisions about housing for the elderly might consider that in new collectivities that are mixed in age, age will be particularly significant. Older people wanting some insulation from categorization in age terms might choose an age-homogeneous community or condominium. In a more abstract sense, individuals aware of variation in age definitions may realize its arbitrariness and decide to try to influence these definitions themselves, as in political efforts to change the retirement age, or even abolish it altogether.

Transitions Across Age Borders

Rites of Passage

Rites of passage are rituals which help individuals move from one known social position to another, and provide signals to the rest of society that this person must now be treated differently. Marriage (single to married), bar mitzvah (boy to man), or funeral (living to ancestor) are all rites of passage. If age marks important boundaries on a social map, then rites of passage will be needed to move people smoothly across them. The presence of elaborate transition rituals is also an indicator of the significance and sharpness of the age boundaries.

The classic pattern for a rite of passage has three stages: separation from the old identity, marginality between two identities, and reincorporation in the new identity. The duration of any of these stages varies from a few minutes or hours to many weeks or months. An American marriage, for instance, includes indicators of separation from the past such as the bride's father "giving her away"; a marginal in-between time on the traditional honeymoon; and reincorporation into society in a new married role on return from the trip. Induction into the armed forces is another example, with more dramatic separation symbols such as head-shaving and stripping of civilian clothes, and a long marginality in training camp before participants reemerge as full-fledged members of the service.

The rites of passage with which some traditional societies move people from one age category to another are famous in ethnographic literature. In the most dramatic, young men are subjected to harrowing physical initiations such as circumcision without anesthetic, and secluded from the rest of society for several weeks, during which they are taught ritual secrets and bullied by their elders. In societies with comprehensive age organizations spanning the entire life course, transitions across several age borders may occur simultaneously at periods of society-wide ritual celebration.

The Masai of Tanzania and Kenya, for example, have six age-grades. Men enter an age-set when they reach adolescence through a series of rituals lasting several months, during which they are secluded from the rest of the village, circumcised, and have their heads shaved by their mothers. Initiations are held every year for four years, followed by a three-year pause, held for another four years followed by another three-year break, at which time the boundary is drawn around an age-set including all those initiated in the fifteen years preceding. These sets are promoted through the grades at fifteen-year intervals, so that when the most recently initiated boys become junior warriors, the set in the junior warrior grade is moved up to senior warriors, and so on.

To keep from obscuring underlying similarity with exotic ethnographic detail, it is important to point out that rites of passage across age borders are not always physically traumatic. The Akwe-Shavante of Central Brazil, for example, have an initiation period lasting over a month during which boys from about twelve to seventeen become men. The rituals of initiation include dunking in cold water, twice daily running exhibitions, dancing, feasting, elaborate body painting, singing at all hours of day or night, and wearing ceremonial masks (Maybury-Lewis 1967). An anthropologist who lived with the Boran of Ethiopia and Kenya, who mark age transitions by changes in hairstyle, feasting, dancing, and singing, argues strongly that these are just as effective as signals of change in age identity as their more painful counterparts in other societies (Legesse 1973b). The essential feature of a rite of passage from this point of view is that it announces to both participants and audience that new social behavior is now required. It is the ensuing change in others' expectations and actions—not the trauma of physical hazing—that gradually shapes the initiates as players of new social roles.

There are other significant cross-cultural variations in age-border crossing. Whether the transition is shared by a group or experienced alone is a basic distinction. If a group is involved in an intense or painful ritual experience and set apart from the rest of society, bonds of solidarity are likely to be created or reinforced. Shared experiences of age-related ritual should stimulate strong ties among age-mates. If a group is involved, another crucial variable is its composition: is the age-group localized, or are age transitions celebrated by individuals from a wide area? Do age ties coincide with many other similarities, such as residence and kinship, or do they cross-cut other bonds?

Ritual passage across age boundaries may also be more or less rigidly timed. In many traditional societies the timing of age-grade transitions is not absolute. Rather than a Mad Hatter's peremptory "Everybody move on!" there is negotiation between pressing younger groups and resisting older, and a gradually mounting tide of de facto graduations, finally recognized in a ritual which also gathers in the stragglers. The Arusha mentioned earlier, for instance, proceed through a smooth flow of individual transitions punctuated and legitimized by official ritual passages.

The Absence of Rites of Passage

How individuals are labelled, and the expectations that those labels engender, have powerful effects both on how people act and on how others treat them. Seen from that point of view, age-boundary rituals are particularly dramatic labelling devices which some societies use to signal new age roles to their occupants and to others. The most distinctive characteristic of rites of passage for American old people is their absence or incompleteness. At most, an older person and the others who have social ties to him or her are offered *exit* signs. The separation phase of a rite of passage may be there in retirement parties or gold watches, but there is no clear pathway back to social reincorporation. The lack of complete transi-

In the rite of passage through which Boran (Kenya) men move into the sacred "retired" age-grade, the old men recount their exploits in a public "life review." (Photo by Asmarom Legesse)

tion rituals is a clear signal only of the lack of clear role definitions for old people in our society. If the consequence of rituals is, as many anthropologists argue, to ease the ambiguity of moments between social roles, then what is the consequence of not having either a ritual *or* a role?

It is no exaggeration to say that this is not a completely human way to live, since human social life consists of discovering, creating, and playing out the orderly patterns represented by social scientists in concepts such as ritual and role. What would we expect human beings confronted with a lack of role or ritual to do? Given our extraordinarily inventive and adaptive history as a species, I would expect them to make some up—which is exactly what some older people are doing. The trip which many people take after retirement, like a honeymoon, provides a spatial symbol of transition, and it may be easier for the retiree and others to shift to new expectations on return from a trip than the day after the retirement party. The rather formal new roles of student or volunteer which some retirees take on as quickly as possible are also ways of clarifying what the society has left ambiguous. A more complete and more profound rite of passage is created by the old people who add the reincorporation stage by entering an age-homogeneous community in which new roles are created by a group of age-mates.

The group versus individual character of a ritual of passage has consequences for ties among age peers. The old people who move together into a new community often feel strong bonds to each other. In the French retirement residence where I spent a year, people arrived in small groups picked up on the same day by the residence chauffeur (Ross, Keith, 1977). These individuals often talked about the closeness they felt to the others who had shared that intensely emotional day of transition. In an American condominium community in California, planners successfully used this principle to foster neighborhood feelings by opening one section of the new condominium at a time, so that a group of about 250 moved together into a spatially distinct area (Byrne 1971, 1974).

Timing of transition rituals also has consequences for the relationships among those on either side of the age boundaries. In a comparative study of over twenty African societies in which age is a very significant aspect of social organization, those with fixed transition rituals were uncommon and did not have conflict between older and younger over transitions. If that pattern is generalized as a hypothesis, we would expect there to be *increasing* conflict over the retirement transition as its timing becomes less fixed.

Conclusion

The clearest conclusion from a comparison of the way age is used to map the life course is that there is great variability. We have seen wide differences in the number of age categories, in the ways they are marked, and in their consistency across individuals and situations. In cross-cultural comparative perspective, the United States is like more traditional societies in some surprising ways and deeply different in others; both have consequences for American old people.

The number of age categories defined, as the Mesakin and

Korongo demonstrate, may have implications for congruity between physical and social age. Many American old people have felt that incongruity sharply in the past; changes in the retirement age may relieve it in the future. More congruence between the age border and individuals crossing it may relieve tension between those on either side.

Americans turn out to be more like most people than is usually assumed in terms of how they perceive the markers of age boundaries. Functional rather than chronological indicators are given priority here, as in most other societies. For one thing this reveals a sharp distinction between official and informal definitions of age, and probably explains why the majority of Americans in the survey were opposed to mandatory retirement. There is more flexibility in definition of age categories, and more openness to individual functional rather than categorical chronological retirement policies than is often thought to be the case.

Age as a principle of categorization must also be seen in the context of other bases of classification in a given social context. In societies where age and other ascriptive criteria are the predominant cues to social interaction, categorization as an old person does not constitute a profound shift in the bases of social differentiation. For many members of societies like the United States, however, the shift to old age is far more than a new status, as the essential means of social identification has also been changed. This shift from priority of achieved to ascribed status is probably felt as a blurring and betrayal of individuality by many older people who have not grown up with ascriptive status. Individual variation in assigning oneself or others to age categories is present in the United States, and these definitions have consequences for how old people view themselves, what they expect from others, including the government, and how others view them.

Situational variation in the definition and salience of age categories is probably more extensive in the United States, or any complex society with its many different domains of social interaction, than in any traditional context. The possible benefit of situational variation is that individuals may have some choice about what situations they spent their time in. Some older people in several modern societies choose to find many different kinds of social satisfaction in a situation where age is irrelevant by living in age-homogeneous communities.

Rites of passage move individuals from one age status to another in many societies. Only the exit phase of these rituals are provided for most older people in our society. Travel after retirement, new formal roles, or moves to retirement communities can be interpreted as older people's inventions of transition rituals. It would be most interesting to study self-imposed symbols of retirement in more detail. Are there shifts in dress or hairstyle, daily routine, speech patterns, leisure activities and the associated equipment, housing, car type or car ownership itself that people use both to announce and to adjust themselves to the transition in age identity?

The cross-cultural comparisons suggest that the timing of transitions affects the relationships between the individuals on either side of the age boundary. When the timing of the transition is less determinate, and consequently a possible topic for negotiation or controversy, there is more likely to be conflict across age lines. From this point of view, a more flexible retirement age should promote age conflict in the United States. In terms of physical and social age congruence, however, conflict should be reduced by retirement flexibility. At this point, the answer is not available. The comparative perspective points out, however, two factors on which our observations should focus if those changes do take place.

Age is used universally, although in diverse ways, to chart a cognitive map of the life course. The next question is how does this map work as a guide? Chapter 3 considers the normative dimension of age borders. Under what conditions and with what consequences are individuals in the same age category expected, by themselves or others, to act or to be treated in certain ways?

Chapter

3

Age
Norms

Norms and ideologies are possible responses to age categorization. Norms are the "oughts" of social life, people's shared feelings about how they and others should behave. Ideologies organize these feelings into more explicit and public systems of ideas about what the world should be like. Individuals categorized together in terms of common age may or may not develop an awareness that their fate is in some way linked, that the way some of them act will affect the others, or that outsiders are likely to treat them all alike. This awareness of participating in a collectivity promotes the development of norms, or ideologies about how members of the collectivity should be treated or should behave. Norm definition and ideological formulation may arise out of either positive or negative evaluation of perceived commonalities. "It's people like that who give us all a bad name," is a reaction revealing feelings of shared fate, although the individuals involved may wish they were not linked together. One possible response to common categorization by age is, of course, that it is not appropriate. As we will see in Chapter 6, some age organizations have as their explicit goal the erasure of age borders. Movements against "agism" as for improved benefits for the elderly are based on ideologies about age—that is, responses to age that become a basis for action in the public domain.

This chapter concentrates on the conditions and consequences of age-related norms. The emphasis is on the situational level. Chapter 4 pursues the issue of age ideologies, and the factors promoting age cleavages in the wider political and economic spheres. Here social, individual, and situational levels are all relevant.

Enforcing Norms

Rewards and Punishments

Old people and young people in the United States disagree very little on norms about how old people should be treated, in particular about who should offer them housing, money, and medical care if they need it. Both see the family as important, but also consider the government an appropriate source of support. What disagreement there is comes from the young people feeling they should offer *more* than the old people are willing to accept (NCOA 1976, p. 222). Support of old people by their children in time of need is clearly a widespread American norm. The more down-to-earth question perhaps concerns sanctions to back up enforcement of the norms. People seem most likely to practice what they preach about good treatment for older relatives in certain circumstances. Enforcement of norms requires first of all an attentive audience to observe behavior, which can then be evaluated as normative or not. An anthropologist who studied the treatment of old people in a small Appalachian community reports that in this face-to-face setting where most families have lived for many generations, a younger person who does not treat an elderly parent well is judged a bad citizen. That negative judgment is possible because members of the community are well known to each other, and it has impact because it affects social responses from the people with whom the individual spends much of his or her social life. Treatment of old people has consequences for their juniors because of how others will judge them, not because the old people themselves control important material resources (Lozier and Althouse 1974). These old people possess the special influence of the supposedly powerless: their condition partly determines the status of the powerful who are responsible for them, e.g., women in many middle Eastern communities, or small children in our own society.

The children of old people who live in a home for old Sephardic Jews in New York receive a similar kind of public acclaim for their good treatment of their elders, in this case made visible in a beautiful, modern building. In the tightly knit ethnic community of New York Sephardim, the expensive, comfortable Home for the Aged is a symbol of the improved social status of the entire group. Contributions to its creation and maintenance are evaluated as significant civic good works, and individual participation is closely monitored by members of the community (Hendel-Sebestyen 1979).

The concept of the "life-term arena" is also relevant to norm enforcement. The individual whose entire life is played out in one social sphere is susceptible to the judgment of the local audience. Among the Chagga of East Africa, about whom anthropologist Sally Falk Moore invented the "life-term arena" concept, failure of a child to care for a parent is disapproved of, just as it has always been. Social change has, however, redefined the agent of enforcement. In the past, the age-grade organization was responsible for monitoring age-related obligations; now it is the socialist political cell in the village which reprimands the young person and makes sure the old person receives care (1978, p. 33).

These examples suggest some characteristics of a situation that predict enforcement of norms for treating old people. The interaction between young and old must be visible to the social audience. Those who know about the young-old relations must have some influence over the young person's life—at a minimum, their opinion must be valued. Treatment of old people must have some salience in the community.

Although it is not surprising that these conditions are present in a traditional Chagga village, or in a close ethnic community in New York, I think it would be a mistake to assume they do not occur in other situations. Increasing numbers of middle-aged Americans stay all their lives very close to where they were born. We know that 75 percent of Americans over sixty-five live within a half-hour of a child; over 50 percent no more than ten minutes away (Shanas 1979). The issue of support for older people is increasingly salient in the society at large. Under these circumstances, it seems likely that caring support of parents will be increasingly a source of "social credit" in American neighborhoods.

Social Clocks: Acting Your Age

"Social clocks" is the phrase used by one group of gerontologists to describe the norms widely shared by Americans about appropriate timing for various life events. There is very high agreement about the best approximate location in the life course for various major roles such as marriage, child rearing, peak career activity, and retirement (Neugarten and Hagestad 1976; Neugarten and Peterson 1957). There are also shared norms, at least among middle-class Americans, about appropriateness at various ages of more specific behaviors such as dress or style of dancing. Researchers in the early 1960s asked whether a person would approve or disapprove such examples as "A woman who feels it's all right at her age to wear a two-piece bathing suit to the beach when she's forty-five? When she's thirty? When she's eighteen?" or "A couple who move across country so they can live near their married children when they're forty? fifty-five? seventy?" They then asked the same people to say what they thought *others* would approve or disapprove.

The answers to these questions showed that many Americans do use age to evaluate appropriateness of behavior, although everyone seems to think that others have more restrictive norms than they do themselves. Similar responses were also obtained in Japan. The older people in both studies voiced the strictest rules about what people of different ages should do, and their personal opinions were more congruent than those of younger people with what they expected others to think. The U.S. researchers also reported that the old people gave their answers with special "vehemence," as though the topic of age norms were "emotionally charged" (Neugarten, Moore, and Lowe 1965; Plath and Ikeda 1975).

Age norms might be especially important to older people for several reasons. Age has powerful implications for their social lives. Fewer other statuses "compete" for priority than in the middle years; and the shift to predominance of an ascriptive categorization is probably a psychological earthquake for many members of an achievement-oriented society like ours.

Creating Age Norms in Old-Age Communities

The importance of age norms to these old people has particular poignancy in view of the lack of clear norms for much of their life stage. The young-old or retired phase of the life course is too new to be clearly defined. Recognition of this new life stage—as opposed to an undifferentiated old age—is increasing, but the details of its content must be filled in by the older individuals who occupy it now.

Highly visible, and therefore potentially highly influential, examples of norm creation by older people occur in the age-homo-geneous communities that have appeared in several industrial societies in the last twenty years. The major hypothesis about the con-ditions under which older people will create norms is Rosow's prop-osition that the necessary context is residential concentration of individuals who share other socially significant characteristics as well as age (1974, pp. 60–62).

Reports from several lively communities of old people with complex and distinctive normative systems prove him right. The French retirement residence in which I lived for a year is one of them, and the emergence of norms was a focus of my observations there (Ross 1977). I will describe Les Floralies in more detail than other communities because I know it up close, but it is not unique. Communities of old people in the United States and in England, in a wide variety of settings ranging from mobile home parks and public housing to luxury condominiums, share many characteristics, including the ways they differ from their surrounding societies (see also Keith 1979).

Certain basic human needs and circumstances must be the subject of normative regulation in any community: death, sex, conflict, and weak or helpless group members must all be managed. The residents of Les Floralies invented and demanded norms about sex and death so clear-cut that even a very young and slightly embarrassed anthropologist couldn't miss them. In fact, explicit admission that death and sex exist and need social responses is in itself a normative difference from the outside society, in which death is generally denied and sex is denied specifically to the old.

Death

The first death at Les Floralies occurred several months after I arrived, and I confess to some ghoulish worries about how I would write an adequate ethnography of an old-age community if no one died. But someone did. The reactions of the old people were set in sharp relief against the attempted nonreaction of the young director. He made no public announcement of the death, moved the body to a basement room, and made no arrangements for transporting residents to the funeral. Rumors that someone was dead were spreading through the dining hall by noon the next day, although there was anxious speculation about who it was. After lunch, many residents dressed up in the clothing that signified response to an important occasion: shoes instead of carpet slippers, suits, gold watches, no aprons. They gathered in the lobby in a group that reminded me of Pirandello's characters in search of an author; they were mourners in search of a funeral. The wife of the president of the Residents Committee led a search party through the building trying to find the body. Others were stationed by the entrances watching for the hearse. The searchers arrived properly solemn but triumphant from the basement to announce they had found the body, and several residents went down to pay last respects. The hearse drove up to the loading ramp outside the basement, and the residents watched the body loaded in, squabbled about who would ride with her, and then saw the driver struggle to gun the heavy car up the steep ramp while the coffin slid out the back.

"I don't want that to happen to me" was the most frequent comment to me about these events; and it was quickly specified that "it" wasn't death, but a bungled social response. Residents of Les Floralies now have what they consider an appropriate response to death, because they demanded it. Through the Residents Committee, they asked that deaths be announced in the dining room and on the bulletin boards, and that transportation to the funeral be provided.

In many other communities, even when old people have not made formal demands about recognition of death they have also created patterns of social support before, during, and after the event. Plans for paying for burial are appropriate topics for discussion, there are shared understandings about being "ready" to go, residents raise money for flowers and attend each other's funerals, and the bereaved are helped back into social interaction in a new single role. All of this is present reassurance to everyone who in the future will certainly be the departed and possibly the bereaved (Hochschild 1973; Marshall 1975).

Sex

If a gerontologist can still shock American nursing home personnel by suggesting that "petting, kissing, or hand-holding would probably go further than a little medication at ten o'clock," sex is not yet an easy subject across age lines. At Les Floralies, sex was certainly considered an appropriate topic for discussion. In even sharper contrast to the world outside, sex was considered an appropriate *activity* for those who wanted it. One of the funnier moments of my fieldwork was a commentary by several old French men and women on a rather patronizing article on the benefits of sex for the elderly in a union newspaper. The old people found this idea less revolutionary than the author apparently did.

Although there is wide variation across cultures in beliefs about appropriate ages for sexual partners, I don't know of any where age is irrelevant. In most Western industrial societies, the norm seems to be for partners of approximately equal age, with any difference in the direction of an older man–younger woman couple. Given the prevailing attitudes in societies like those of the United States and France, it seems probable that most old people, like the residents of Les Floralies, will talk about sex most comfortably, and instructively, among themselves. Love and romance may also be difficult to reveal to many young people, for fear of shock or ridicule at worst, patronization at best. The occasional "senior citizen wedding" pictures with their clever captions are not reassuring. If being considered cute is the best an older couple can hope for from their juniors, they may prefer to remain in the closet.

There are also specific norms about sexual relationships at Les Floralies. Men and women who share domestic arrangements, appear together publicly, and are presumed to have a sexual relationship are

"It's a second life for us," was the description of their relationship by this French couple who met in a retirement residence near Paris. (Photo by Marc Ross)

"married" in the eyes of other residents, even if not in the eyes of French law, and are addressed as Mr. and Mrs. There is wide understanding of reasons for living together without marriage: "What would the children think?" or loss of widow's pension benefits, for example. Dead spouses were discussed freely between and in front of new couples, although jealousy of living rivals was intense. Promiscuity is disapproved not because it involves sex, but only if it threatens to create conflict (a married man pawing other women at a dance) or to "give the residence a bad name" (a man who brought a whore and her pimp to his room on the invalid's floor) (Ross 1977).

Families

Children are much on the minds of many residents in more positive ways than speculation about their reaction to sex and romance. In spite of many false notions to the contrary, the old people in age-homogeneous communities are not all childless or estranged from children who "put" them there. About 50 percent of the residents in the communities for which we have information have children. When distance is controlled for, these old people have as much contact with their children as those living elsewhere (Sherman 1975). Shared norms and values about relationships with children are a central feature of the cultures created in old-age communities.

First of all, children are included in many community activities. Christmas was rescheduled at Les Floralies so that residents could celebrate in their children's homes and also invite their children to the community. Sundays the dining room always buzzed with grandchildren, who knew after a few visits which tables were the most reliable sources of candy. Families participate in various festivities in many American communities and, as in France, there are clear norms about paying for guests who eat meals or party refreshments (Johnson 1971).

The most frequent complaint I hear from the children of old people in various communities is that it's difficult to get in touch with them because they are so busy. There is often an air of rather indignant surprise that grandma is not available on demand. In fact, the old people usually share norms about priorities of socializing, so that it is understood that a visit from a child, even an unexpected one, takes precedence over an activity with another resident, with no hurt feelings (Jonas 1979). Children's and grandchildren's lives are also major conversation topics, and plans to visit with them are shared (e.g., Hochschild 1973).

Peer ties not only do not conflict with family bonds, but may even be linked with them in a more positive way. Among residents in old-age communities, the individuals most involved in peer networks are also most in contact with their kin (Jonas 1979; Ross 1977). The main explanation for the nonsubstitutability of peer and kin ties is that they are qualitatively different (Rosow 1967, p. 217ff). The quality of both may even be improved by their coexistence. Less dependence on children may make both parents and children more relaxed and ready to enjoy less duty-bound encounters (Talmon 1968; Neugarten and Hagestad 1976). A little griping among understanding friends may also be an escape valve for tensions: being last in line for the family bathroom was a topic for joking commiseration when Les Floralies residents returned from weekend visits. Restrictions on family visits to the community, such as number of days or hours when children may use the pool, are also imposed by the collectivity rather than by the individual old person, which may be a relief in several senses.

Mutual Aid

Members of old-age communities help each other in more personalized ways as well. At Les Floralies, as in many American residences, there are individuals who are quite literally supported through their daily lives by friends they have made since moving there. A blind woman helped to dress, eat, and walk to public activities or a very frail resident carefully assisted to every meal are particularly memorable examples, but the norm of mutual aid is played out less dramatically daily in every old people's community I know of. In a tri-ethnic public housing complex in Florida, for instance, an anthropologist discovered what she calls "health protector" pairs, in which a stronger resident takes general responsibility for the well-being of someone more frail (Kandel and Heider 1979). In other residences, the old people invent check-up schemes to be sure no one is ill or injured alone: if shades are not up by ten A.M., a neighbor knocks; if a table-mate does not appear in the dining room, someone visits their room.

A particularly discreet form of social support which might be labelled "aid without intimacy" appears in big city "single room occupancy" hotels. This rather sordid setting for community is a reminder of its weed-like tendency to appear in even the most repressive or arid circumstances. SRO's, once considered the epitome of urban anomie, have recently been studied intensively by several researchers who have found social networks among the residents and the staff of the hotels. There are norms of mutual aid, but also additional norms about the conditions under which aid may be sought or given without development of an intimacy which most of these loners have fled all their lives (Eckert 1980; Erickson and Eckert 1977; Sokolovsky and Cohen, 1978, 1981).

The norm of mutual aid in most old-age communities is strong, and has much to do with the feelings that many old people have expressed to me in terms of fictional kinship: "they are my residence family." But help is not extended to everyone. In the French residence, it went to members of the appropriate political faction. What is significant about this is not the political aspect, but that the individuals receiving help were known community members whose helpers felt linked to them by a strong bond. I have seen the same people who offered extensive help to a member of the community stare stonily at a helpless newcomer arriving at the residence. The bitter suggestion from one unwelcoming onlooker was: "why not save time and take her right to the basement [where the morgue room is]?" Residents expressed fears that too many impaired newcomers would turn their community into an institution.

Physical and Mental Infirmity

Deep fears of physical disability and senility are met in two opposite ways. Either afflicted individuals are helped, which allows them to participate in community life and not threaten it; or they are rejected, and treated as nonmembers. The commonsensical distinction I have observed is between those to whom residents have existing ties and those to whom they don't. Strong social ties develop very quickly in these communities, which offers a practical suggestion to those considering a move to one. Moving in *before* a major physical crisis offers a strong possibility that by the time such an event occurs there will be a supportive network of friends to ease it. Arrival as a handicapped person, and probably spatial separation in some euphemistically labelled but stigmatized invalid wing or floor, is likely to prevent those ties from ever developing.

Equality

In contrast to the norm of supporting weaker residents, there is in old-age communities also a norm that could be described as pulling down those who are too strong. A more positive description is that there is a powerful norm of equality in terms of external statuses. At Les Floralies, such outside indicators of social status as occupation, income, health, or age itself are simply irrelevant to status inside the residence. In the United States, members of one California community deposed from their Board of Managers a resident who bought two of the nearly identical condominium units and linked them by a covered walk in a more imposing residence that he felt suited his status as a former stock exchange executive. The explicit explanation for his removal from political office was that "We're all old people here; it doesn't matter what you were before" (Hill 1968). Almost the same words came from residents of a public housing complex in California, where the president of the Residents Council seemed to be putting on airs after invitations to lunches with other civic leaders. "Who does she think she is? We're all elder people here" (Hochschild 1973). Members of the California condominium mentioned above also strongly resisted the publication of a Who's Who which would present information about people's previous lives. The resistance was not to making the information available—in this little community, people already knew it. They resisted the emphasis and implied significance given to that past-tense information by such a publication.

Homophily: "Birds of a Feather . . ."

"Old people are people" recurs as a theme in Rosow's statement of his proposition that residential concentration will promote norm definition by old people (1974). As he points out, the principle of *homophily* suggests that most people turn to others like them to meet major social needs. To suggest that older people are likely to find friends, to create viable groups, and to define norms when they have access to age-mates is only to say that they are likely to act like other people, and for the same reasons. The homophily principle implies that old people should create communities and norms when they share the spatial context for community with others who have in common with them major social characteristics in addition to age. The community studies so far available generally support this proposition. Most housing for older people is homogeneous in many ways. Income is filtered by minimums in private housing, by maximums in public housing. Self-selection and sponsorship also produce many similarities in ethnicity, religion, and life-style. Most residents do not move far from their previous homes, so region is often shared. Demographic facts of life promote high degrees of homogeneity in sex and marital status: widowed women predominate in most communities. One refinement of the homogeneity factor in community formation is provided by studies of multiethnic American public housing. Communities do form in these contexts, although the level of community feeling and integration does not seem to be as high as in the more homogeneous settings. Strong communal bonds develop in subgroups, however, as in buildings within a public housing complex that are highly homogeneous in terms of ethnicity and marital status to begin with, and are then linked by individuals or by desirable organized events like hot meals or bus excursions (Kandel and Heider 1979; Wellin and Boyer 1979).

Non-Western Age Collectivities

An important expansion of the "old people are people" theme in terms of norms is to a broader cross-cultural view of age collectivities and their norms. In other words, what do these groups have in common with Western old-age communities? Age-mates in many traditional societies also share norms about sex, death, mutual aid, and equality.

Sex

The most common understanding about sex among age-mates is that it may be shared: although the daughters of men in the same age-set are not usually available sexual partners—"it would be like your own daughter"—girlfriends and wives often are. Among the

Arusha, age-mates have the privilege of sexual access to each other's wives, as long as this doesn't occur often enough to threaten the couple. In Mandan Indian society: "On some nights all the members (of an age society) sent for their wives. Then water was poured on the fire, and in the darkness each man seized and hugged someone else's wife" (Lowie 1913, p. 266).

In a comparative cross-cultural study, an expert on African age organization showed the relationship between presence of formal age-sets and permission of premarital promiscuity for men (Legesse 1973a). In the different societies, younger men not yet eligible for marriage are permitted to have sex with various partners—young married women, older married women, widows, divorcees, or age-mates of the same sex. What is common in all the systems is that sex is somehow regulated by the age organization, and that there are appropriate norms for sexual behavior by and among age-mates.

Demography plus the changing *youthful* sexual experiences of old people in our future may combine in more inventive sexual norms. The premarital sexual arrangements of the traditional age organizations might be paralleled by postmarital arrangements which permit several old women to share one of the scarce old men. In communities of old people, this kind of norm would be the old people's own business, and consequently may not be a distant fantasy. A more radical shift would be to general acceptance by young and old alike of young men and older women as appropriate sexual partners. The parallel to the traditional examples would be a norm approving such ties as temporary liaisons but not as bases for marriage.

Death

Age-mates also traditionally attend to each other's deaths. They usually have specific responsibilities in funerals, often paying some costs or, as among the Hidatsa Indians, giving food and gifts to the bereaved as well (Stewart 1977, p. 277). Nuer age-sets are unusual because their rule is the reverse: age-mates must not bury each other, and must not even eat meat at one another's funeral feasts. Direct reversal of many other rules is less of an exception than no rule at all: what is common is some normative response to death among age-mates.

Mutual Aid

Mutual aid in life as well as at death is reported among age-set or age-group members around the world. The Hidatsa, for example, contributed money if an age-mate wanted to perform a costly ritual, restrained him if his participation in ceremonial self-torture was too risky, and gave assistance in terms of economic stress, such as theft of his horses. In many African societies, age-mates help an individual obtain the cattle for the required gift to his bride's family. This kind of support persists in modern contexts also, as among the Atié of the Ivory Coast, who pool their money within an age-set to buy a taxi which they operate collectively.

Equality

Egalitarianism is a very widespread norm for relations among age-mates in out-of-power age-grades, probably as a counterbalance to the hierarchy implicit in relations across age boundaries. Like the residents of modern retirement communities, members of many traditional age-sets are under great social pressure not to stand out from their peers, especially in terms of external standards (e.g., within a warrior grade, exceptional skill as a warrior is less objectionable than unusual wealth).

Among the Nuer, age-mates "are on terms of entire equality. A man does not stand on ceremony with his age-mates, but jokes, plays, and eats with them at his ease. Age-mates associate in work, war, and in all the pursuits of leisure. They are expected to offer one another hospitality and to share their possessions" (Evans-Pritchard 1940; rpt. 1968, p. 258). Equality is guarded in some systems by shifting out of a set individuals who are markedly stronger or weaker, e.g., Bartle Bay, New Guinea; Nuba and Masai, East Africa (Stewart 1977). In nineteenth century Swiss *Jahrgangervereine,* any member who inherited a large estate, made a wealthy marriage, or was otherwise "especially favored by fortune" had to make a special contribution to the age-group (Trümpy 1965, cited in Stewart 1977, p. 338). The Arusha recognize influential individuals who become visible as an age-set moves up the grades, but these people must be very cautious not to neglect ". . . egalitarian obligations to age-mates or incline toward authoritarian neglect of their interests or opinions" (Gulliver 1963, p. 52). Anyone too unmindful of egalitarian values is rapidly reminded of them—like the conspicuous consumer who lost his place on the California condominium board, such a person loses influence and has no choice but to be once again equal to his peers. One already influential member of a senior Arusha age-grade was very uneasy when, because of his position in the traditional system, he was given the right to vote in the 1958 Tanganyika national elections. More sensitive than the California Resident's Council president who irritated her constituents by enjoying her outside recognition too much, he feared being judged "overambitious and presumptuous." His solution was to ask for approval from the age-set before registering to vote, and promising that he would poll his age-mates and vote as they directed (Gulliver 1963, p. 49).

The reasons that anthropologists have hypothesized for these traditional norms of equality may illuminate the behavior of old people in their new communities. In most traditional systems, one age-grade, usually that of adolescence and youth, is more elaborated than the others (Gulliver 1968). Typically, the occupants of that grade are *told* that these are the best years of their lives (like our comments to retired people about the enviability of their leisure?). Although the young men wear fancy clothes, dance, and make love, they are totally excluded from decision making and ownership of most important resources. This grade has been compared by one anthropologist to British boarding schools, which he thinks perform a similar kind of holding action for youths whose entrance to social maturity and power is delayed while they are told they are enjoying the best years of their lives (Spencer 1965). Under these circumstances, refusal to allow outside status in provides some insulation from an outside system in which the age-mates are by definition losers. The parallel to our old-age communities seems to me very clear: the promotion of equality inside is a protection against inequality outside. This interpretation suggests that invocation of common age as a reason for equality should be most likely among age-sets which are not in powerful positions—in our society, for example, most common before and after the middle years (Almagor 1978). It may also be more likely in societies where there is an "official" cultural imperative for equality, as in modern democracies or socialist states, less likely in contexts where inequality is considered an appropriate state of affairs, as in a caste-ordered society like India or Indonesia.

Factors Contributing to the Development of Distinctive Age Norms

"New norms or used?" is the broader question raised by the issue of status contrasts inside and outside age groups. If old people in age-homogeneous communities create norms, when will these be distinctive from those of the wider society and when will the norms be parallel? Both could offer some protection from a loser's position in the outside status system, but new, distinctive norms are a stronger shield, and would also have more potential for social change through influence on old people outside the new communities.

Rosow's answer to his own question about when norms defined by old people in separate residential settings will be distinctive is, when these entities are viable groups. For them to become positive reference groups in *nonyouthful* terms, they would also have to be viable social groups that serve other major functions for their members (1974, p. 160). "Viable group" suggests as a first broad hypothesis that the higher the level of community achieved among the old people living together, the more likely that their shared norms will be distinctive.

Returning to the "old people are people" refrain, examination of old people's communities in comparison with many other examples of community creation suggests some more specific hypotheses about the relationship between norms inside and out. There are three broad possibilities for this relationship: (1) The inside social organization in all aspects may be as far as possible a reflection of the outside. Inmates of a women's prison in West Virginia, for instance, recreated a detailed version of an American kinship system, including spouses, children, siblings, cousins, aunts, and uncles—and appropriate norms of reciprocal behavior (Giallombardo 1966). (2) Inside norms may represent a reaction against some aspect of the outside world. Hutterites, for example, have organized independent communities called *Bruderhof,* where members of the sect are dedicated explicitly to overcoming the individualistic, materialist, violent values they feel dominate the wider American society (Hoestetler and Huntington 1967). Many utopian experiments are based on this kind of reaction, expressed in a "last shall be first" reversal of worldly values. (3) The outside significance of any social condition may also simply be refused, so that it becomes irrelevant within the new community. The resistance to external social status in retirement communities is an example. Either reversal or irrelevance produces more distinctive norms than reflection, although reversal seems more tied to the outside than irrelevance.

Comparison of various types of communities produces some hypotheses about factors that in various combinations make one of these patterns more likely than another: (1) consensus versus disagreement in evaluation of a particular attribute by insiders and outsiders; (2) intentionality of community creation; and (3) residents' expectations of temporary versus permanent membership in it.

Norms that make outside patterns irrelevant are most likely when there is disagreement in evaluation of the characteristics shared by new community members, when community creation is unintentional, and when members anticipate staying for a very high proportion of their lives. This combination of factors is typical of most old-age communities. Older people's evaluations of old age differ from those of younger people. Most old people do not move to age-homogeneous residences *intentionally* in search of community. They look for affordable housing, for security, and independence; community is what they find, not what they were seeking. "We're here for the rest of our lives" is a very common statement of the permanent commitment most old people feel to their new communities. There is a mixture of hope and resignation in those statements, but they express a deep commitment to the new situation.

These specific patterns reinforce Rosow's hypothesis that *if* a viable group, or a high level of community, develops in an age-homogeneous residential context, *then* distinctive norms for old age should emerge.

"Norms for whom?" is the next question: under what conditions might norms created by old people in separate communities, still a very small proportion of the older population, spread out to influence other present or future elderly? The degree of choice that people perceive in making decisions is seen by social psychologists as an important predictor of how they will justify their actions, which in turn is an important factor in norm creation. The justifications people give for *past* actions, in other words, often become reasons for similar actions in the future. The element of choice people perceive is crucial, because if they feel constrained by external forces they do not need to justify their actions any further than by pointing out that constraint, and the norm creation process is cut off (Kiesler 1981).

Two changes should produce this result. First, as the positive social aspects of old-age communities become better known, these will become reasons for choosing to live there. This will be a less externally constrained reason than the difficulty of preserving independence and security in "normal" neighborhoods, which is now the most common justification. Second, older people's incomes have improved significantly in recent years and future health legislation should increase their protection. Choice of a retirement community in that context should also be perceived as somewhat less constrained, leading to justification in terms of its intrinsic rather than forced reasonableness.

The Consequences of Creating Norms

Norms to guide social life are part of the human situation. Many researchers have argued, Rosow most eloquently of all, that American society does not provide norms and roles for old age, so that old people have a choice between scrambling harder and harder to meet youthful norms and an inhuman ambiguity of normlessness.

A lonely bench on Coney Island's boardwalk symbolizes the situation of many isolated old Americans. (Photo by Jay Sokolovsky)

Evidence from comparisons of old people living in age-homogeneous and mixed-age situations shows that those in old-age communities have higher morale than those living with younger people (Bultena 1974). The reason is probably that they share norms. Support for that interpretation comes from the fact that it is not simply more social activity that explains this higher satisfaction with life. Although old people in age-homogeneous settings do have more social activity, the higher morale levels are independent of amount of activity (Teaff, Lawton, and Carlson 1977). This is very reasonable in light of individual differences in lifelong patterns of social participation, and in amount of desired activity. Old people do not all want the same amounts or kinds of social activity. The relationship between availability of age-peers and higher morale still needs explanation, however, and the development of norms is the most persuasive.

Conclusion

The situation of age-homogeneous residence promotes development of both the social and the emotional aspects of community. The higher the level of community, the more likely that distinctive norms will emerge; and specific patterns of norm definition inside these communities follow those of many other examples of community formation. Availability of these norms seems to promote higher morale among old people. Choosing to live in an old-age community as itself a positive norm among older people seems likely in the future, according to social psychological theories of choice and norm definition.

Expansion of these normative questions from the small scale of retirement communities out into the wider society continues in Chapter 4. There the focus is on ideological responses to age categorization in broader political and economic domains.

Chapter

4

Battles at the Age Border? Age Ideology and Intergenerational Conflict

Responses to age categorization may also trace ideological boundaries through a society: individuals in various age categories may be aware of that collective identity in ways that define shared beliefs about the *appropriate* significance of age, or about various political and economic issues affecting their age category. There are many hypotheses about the conditions under which age acquires ideological significance, in particular about when age becomes a boundary of conflict. As if the intangible nature of the ideological topic were contagious, most of these hypotheses are on a high level of abstraction, dealing with characteristics of entire societies, or large chunks of historical time. In addition, there are far more hypotheses than empirical data with which to evaluate them. Scholarly interest in age ideology itself seems to follow a historical pattern, a reminder that research questions as well as their answers may be indicators of age as a social border.

Social Change and Age Ideology

A very basic characteristic of any society is its degree of stability. Social change is the factor most persistently proposed as a cause of ideological age differentiation. The key concept in these proposals is generation, which has two distinct meanings. It may refer to *genealogical* relations of senior and junior—for example, regardless of chronological age, the sons of a set of brothers are the junior generation, their father and his brothers are the senior. Generation is also used to refer to an *age* category, as in Western society people often speak of the younger or older generation (Kertzer 1981). The two usages may coincide if members of a genealogical generation are of roughly the same age. Factors such as large family size, or polygyny may, however, force the two progressively farther apart (Legesse 1973b).

Mannheim's Concept of Generation

Generation is usually used in discussions of age ideology in the sense of relative age rather than of genealogical categories. Although it was not the first, Karl Mannheim's essay on "The Problems of Generations" has been both the stimulus and the benchmark for most subsequent work on the topic (1952). Mannheim first distinguishes generation as a social entity from the biological flow of individuals through age categories. Membership in a generation is based on similar age *and* location in the same historical community. In other words, a generation must be considered in a social context. Next, Mannheim introduces the idea of generation as an "actuality" which is constituted when individuals who share a historical location are also exposed to, and react to, social and intellectual currents characteristic of their society and period. Finally, he defines the *generation unit* as those age-mates who share the *same* responses to their historical situation. A generation unit has a concrete group as its nucleus, but its characteristic attitudes may spread out from that point of origin, so the boundary around the unit is ideological rather than interactional. In explicit parallel to Marxian interpretations of class, the generation unit is a generation *for* itself, in contrast to the generation in actuality, or *in* itself.

The tempo of social change is the cause of generation unit formation, according to Mannheim. Changes in the society expose members of an age category to experiences different enough from those of their seniors that they become aware of the distinctiveness of their experience. That awareness, combined with their shared responses to the specific changes they encounter, then leads to their sharing attitudes about existing aspects of the society and hence to demands for further changes. The point missed in many later discussions is Mannheim's suggestion that the relationship between rate of social change and age ideology is curvilinear: up to a certain point, the faster the rate of change, the more likely it is that generation units will form; but after that point, if the tempo of change increases too much, the responses of different age categories will be "so closely packed together that they do not succeed in . . . formulation of distinct generational [ideologies]" (1952, p. 310). Many later studies simply refer to a link between rapid change and generational polarization, but without the refinement of Mannheim's emphasis on curvilinearity (cf. Feuer 1969; Foner 1972; Davis 1940). One who took exception to this, as she did to so many other generalizations, was Margaret Mead, who acknowledged the curvilinear effects of change when she wrote about change leading to "cofigurative" or "prefigurative" patterns of socialization. In a cofigurative pattern, learning from peers is very important because change has made the experiences of older people an inadequate basis of socialization for the young. Prefigurative learning appears when change is so pervasive that the old must learn from the young (1970).

Change as a variable affecting age ideology is, in short, typically not seen as variable enough. There is important variation not only in rate of change, but also in type and domain of change. The sheer bulk and impressiveness of a historical event is likely to elicit feelings of collectivity from members of an age category who experience it at the same time in their lives. A war or a depression produces shared feelings of "we were there and no one else can really understand" that persist through people's lives (Elder 1975; Rosow 1978). These seem to be a different order of feelings than those elicited by even very rapid change in technology, for example. The timing of "bulges" of scientific interest in age ideology seems to correspond to these kinds of particularly impressive historical events. Mannheim's original formulation came after World War I; Davis's and Parsons's after World War II; and the most recent surge of interest after the civil rights movement and Vietnam War of the 1960s (Laufer and Bengtson 1974).

Revivalistic change, as a type distinct from more forward moving social alterations, was discussed in Chapter 1 as having quite different effects on the status of old people—for example, among the Coast Salish Indians. Revivalistic change might also have distinctive effects on age ideology, since it is likely to define a boundary between those rediscovering the old ways and those who remember them on one hand, and those in the middle who neither know nor want to know them, on the other.

Bateson's Concept of Schismogenesis: Types of Change

A set of propositions by Gregory Bateson about types of change and their effects on social differentiation in general can be translated into the specific case of age ideology. Bateson's "schismogenesis" theory was developed in the 1930s to analyze the various possible responses to contacts between cultures, such as were occurring in many colonial situations. His argument is that different kinds of contacts across social borders lead to increased differentiation (schismogenesis) or to maintenance of status quo. The three kinds of boundary relations he identifies are symmetrical, complementary, and reciprocal. *Symmetrical* relationships exist when both internal and external behaviors and attitudes on both sides of the border are similar; his examples are gangs, which behave similarly toward each other and whose behavior inside their borders is also of mirror image similarity. *Complementary* relationships occur when both internal and external behaviors of each category are fundamentally different: across the border, one is authoritative, one is deferent; within the border, one is hierarchical, one is egalitarian. British colonial administrators of a traditional African tribal society would be an example. Bateson calls both the symmetrical and the complementary patterns schismogenic: unless certain restraining forces are present, these patterns of interaction lead to increasing differentiation and conflict. *Reciprocity* in contacts across a border, on the other hand, does not promote schismogenesis (Bateson 1967).

The restraints of increasing differentiation are: an admixture of symmetrical and complementary relations, such as a ritual rebellion; development of mutual dependence, such as trade of material necessities; presence of some reciprocal elements; and opposition to some force external to both categories. Increasing presence of these factors should restrain schismogenesis; removal of any of them should make differentiation more likely.

Complementarity and Polarization. Translated into our terms of age differentiation, Bateson's scheme offers many specific hypotheses about types of change that should promote or suppress distinctive age ideologies. Changes that make relations across an age border less reciprocal and more symmetrical or complementary should make age polarization more likely. Changes stimulating reciprocity, or introducing more restraining factors should make age ideologically less significant. For example, old people in a public housing project administered by a bureaucracy such as the Department of Housing and Urban Development (HUD) participate in *complementary* relations. The old people's ties to each other are likely to be highly egalitarian, as we saw in Chapter 3; HUD is hierarchically organized, like any bureaucracy. Housing and Urban Development staff have authority over the old people, and often feel a paternalistic responsibility for them (Kandel and Heider 1979). The old people must be obedient to HUD rules and, at least superficially, respectful of their caretakers. A nursing home and its staff provide a more extreme example. Age ideologies do arise in these situations. Personnel who deal with old people often share beliefs about how old people need to be or may be treated—quite differently from patients or renters of different ages. In public housing, the staff makes decisions "for the old people's own good," for example, having rules against bingo or gambling games or minimizing public response to a death (Kandel and Heider 1979). It is also possible to forbid residents to organize any group activities that might cause difficulties for the manager (cf. Francis 1981). In nursing homes, it is possible to call adults, if they are old, by their first names, to ignore their desire for privacy in bathing or using the toilet, even to the extent of mixing men and women in showers (Kayser-Jones 1981; Gubrium 1975).

Age ideology develops from the other side of the border as well, as we saw in the discussion of old-age communities. Opposition to policies of the director of Les Floralies, for example, was characteristically phrased in terms of his youthfulness. Resentment against the *in loco parentis* attitude of some HUD officials is also phrased in terms of age by residents themselves old enough to be the parents of those "whippersnappers." "I can't wait 'til you're old!" was the retort of one angry resident to a patronizing recreation director in California (Hochschild 1973, p. 130).

Reciprocity. Bateson's restraining factors also seem to operate across age boundaries. In a comparison of a Scottish nursing home with one in California, for example, a medical anthropologist felt that the Scottish old people were treated far better for several reasons that could fit into Bateson's "reciprocal" category. In an occupational therapy group, the Scots made items, such as knitted sweaters, which had significant value to staff members. The items were offered as gifts or sold at low prices by the old people to members of the staff, who consequently had something to gain by good treatment and something to lose by alienation of their patients. The old people in Scotland also controlled small amounts of money, with which they bought candy or cakes at the home's shop; these were also small, but desirable favors given to the nursing staff. The Americans had no creative activity and no homemade objects to give away; they were also unable to keep money in their rooms, since it might be stolen. As Bateson's theory predicts, the descriptions of the two settings reveal more individualized response to the Scottish old people, and an ideology of infantilizing the old in the American home.

Old-age communities, public housing for the old, and nursing homes are all recent social phenomena. Social changes have produced these contexts in which complementary relations across the age boundary occur. The age ideologies developed in these settings are also spreading back out to the wider society: in the paternalistic, social problems approach to old people, and in their response of ideologies that either demand rights based on age, or a "nonagist" reduced emphasis on age differentiation.

Bateson's other types of cross-border contact and other restraints on conflict offer a guide to further investigation of age borders and age ideology. An added advantage of his framework is that it was *not* created specifically for study of age, and certainly not of old age. The theoretical implication of our "old people are people" theme is that it is desirable to integrate studies of old age into more general theories of human behavior, and that what we learn from old people contributes to the refinement of those theories and our understanding of human social life in general.

Age Bias in Research

There is, perhaps ironically, a strong age bias in research on age ideology. Although hypotheses are stated in general terms of age or generation boundaries, until very recently they have all in fact referred to young ages and younger generations. Distinctive contact with change, fresh reactions to it, new ideas to teach to other age categories are assumed—not demonstrated—to be the prerogative of the young. Communities of old people and their political organizations, as well as old-age political issues such as mandatory retirement and Medicare have stimulated more recent studies of possible generation units among the old (Ragan and Dowd 1974).

In a very simple but profound sense, certain social changes must be experienced by the old first. Changes having to do with the later years of life necessarily will be known and responded to first by the old. The stretching out of life itself, with the resulting definition of a new "young-old" or "retired" life stage, is the most essential example. In precisely the terms of "fresh contact" with change that Mannheim uses to predict generation units among the young, we should expect them among the old, who are moving through this new life stage in front of the rest of us.

Part of the "freshness" to which Mannheim refers is supposed to come from younger people's encountering social changes before they are deeply enmeshed in the social commitments of the middle years. Those roles and responsibilities are assumed to have a conservative influence, leading to resistance to change or to attempts to redirect it in a less radical direction. If the variable itself—involvement in many responsible social roles—is separated from assumptions about life stages at which that involvement occurs, it is clear that in some societies, such as our own, the hypothesis should predict "fresh contact" for older and retired people as well as for the young. We should expect, then, "shared moral views and demands for change" from older people.

The unidirectional hypotheses about effects of extreme social change on intergenerational learning also need review for possible age bias. Mead suggested that in times of greatest change, the old must learn from the young. Mannheim also proposed that in dynamic times, the young would become the teachers. If the change affects the later stages of life, however, the old will be the teachers; and the more radical the change, the more unique and necessary their expertise. It seems quite appropriate to reinterpret Margaret Mead in these terms; as an old woman she taught many of us a great deal in very dynamic times.

Attention to development of age ideology among the old as well as the young also points out a rigid linearity in most views of generational alignments. The focus on youth, and factors that should foster distinctive social responses among them, suggests that the only possible generational alignments are the young with or against every one else. As Mannheim pointed out long ago, another possible line-up of age boundaries, especially in times of change, is the young and the old against those in the middle. In cross-cultural terms, the alternative generation alliance is very common (Apple 1956). Many formal age-grade systems have this kind of two-stream loyalty (Spencer 1976). The Gray Panthers, who attempt to ally the young and the old in response to, and demands for, social change, are in this sense reviving a widespread and traditional system.

Resistance to Age Borders:
Cross-Cutting Ties

The explicit proposition that age opposition is most likely in the absence of other social ties cross-cutting the age borders has been made by many researchers (e.g., Gulliver 1968; Foner 1972; Hess 1972). In another return to the "old people are people" refrain, this is of course a basic principle of social life. When many interests or identities coincide, a conflict is likely to follow the line along which they overlap; but individuals who are joined to each other by some identities and linked to members of other social categories in other ways are less likely to line up together in a faction (Coleman 1957). In age terms, the argument is that an ideology focused on age would emerge with great difficulty among individuals who are in the same age-grade but are divided by other major roles such as occupation and kinship. Although there are in complex societies many differences among people before and after these major midlife roles, there are in relative terms fewer social ties cross-cutting age identity than in the middle years.

A more ideological hypothesis about age ideology, which accounts for its predominance outside the middle years in many societies, both traditional and modern, is that age is a particularly appropriate structural vehicle for egalitarian values. Age does not cause egalitarianism, in other words, but is a very effective way of expressing and protecting it. This would explain the difficulty of maintaining age ties during the time of life when in many societies people are most unequal (Almagor 1978a). It would suggest also that age ideology should be invoked by those who are on the bottom in status battles, and therefore stand to gain by a pressure for equality. The striking parallels between old-age communities and warrior age-sets support this. Finally, age ideology should be dominant throughout life only in societies which are highly egalitarian. The cross-cultural evidence supports this: (1) in most societies, age ideology is not consistently significant across the life span; and (2) the classic examples of comprehensive age organization, such as Masai, are vehemently egalitarian.

Age may also be outweighed by a more powerful unifying principle, such as war or catastrophe. Like any potentially divisive social border, age should be temporarily overruled in a community confronted by an external threat, either human or force of nature. The combination of this solidarity in the face of threat with the hypothesis that response to vast historical events promotes age ideologies predicts a reduced emphasis on age differences during the episode, then an emphasis of age differences in the ensuing responses to it.

Reinforcement of Age Borders: Spatial Separation

Physical or spatial separation of different age categories is seen as a source of "age polarization" by Riley and her associates in their general theory of age stratification (1972, p. 447). In interesting opposition to this is the interpretation of spatial separation in several traditional societies where it is seen by both the members of these communities and the anthropologists who study them as a means of *reducing* age conflict. Living in perhaps the most famous traditional example of "age villages," the Nyakyusa of Tanzania, for instance, believe that boys should cultivate the "good company" of their age-mates, eating and sleeping with them in separate villages from the age of about ten. These villages, to which first girlfriends and eventually wives come to join the men, are seen by the Nyakyusa as a means of avoiding conflict between fathers and sons who otherwise might compete over the young wives of the polygynous older men (Wilson 1951).

The joys of grandma's kitchen reflect the affectionate ties between grandparent and grandchild that appear in most of the world's societies. (Photo by Jennie Keith)

Separate Quarters and Reduced Conflict

As we saw in Chapter 3, separate housing or separate localities for age categories are not uncommon around the world. The usual interpretation of the effects of this separation is that it reduces conflict across age boundaries (Skinner 1961; Paulme 1973). However, the ultimate resolution of these opposing views of spatial separation will require data that are not now available about the consequences of separate residence for age relations in modern society. Although there are examples of old people in the United States fighting for their right to live in age-homogeneous communities, there is no evidence I know of that living with age-mates is a *source* of intergenerational conflict.

Even though the argument cannot be resolved with the information we have now, the data bring out several useful points. Once

This father and son planting corn in a Central Mexican village may one day face each other in a courtroom to dispute transfer of the land from older to younger generation. (Photo by Jay Sokolovsky)

again, there is not a clear traditional-modern split on an important issue. Conflict between generations is not a modern invention; it occurs in many traditional settings, where the significant difference may be in their invention of ways to manage it. The parallels we have already observed between age-sets in some traditional societies and the old-age communities recently created in modern contexts also suggest that there may be the further similarity that this spatial concentration of age-mates reduces rather than promotes conflict with other age categories.

First, as we saw in Chapter 3, the norms of support and the social opportunities among age peers may relieve the family of the stresses of being sole provider of both material and emotional needs for the older person. On a more abstract level, formalized and collective relations between generations may also ease conflict. A social structural balancing act between the vertical pull of kinship and the horizontal bonds of age occurs in many societies; and it is typically the kinship domain that is perceived as the villain, or source of disharmony. The stressful fact that children replace parents is, of course, universal. The issue here is whether that same generational relationship writ large into age-grades and sets might ease the strain by containing family conflicts so that they cannot expand through a community, or by relieving some of the strain within the kin group.

Some Cross-Cultural Examples

Central Brazil. In Central Brazil, the Indian worldview emphasizes duality. The distinction between the sexes is highly elaborated; villages are divided into central and peripheral areas; the cosmos is seen as pushed and pulled toward equilibrium by opposing forces of harmony and strife. These various dualities come together in the complementarity of kinship and age affiliations. Although specifics differ, there is a general theme of kinship as conflictual and the age organization as a harmonious counterweight. Village centers are male spheres, where formal, public activities take place. The center is the ritual domain, and issues reach the political agenda through introduction in the men's forum there. The periphery is the female world, where households are located, and domestic, private life goes on. The age organization operates in the center, sometimes in opposition to kinship at the periphery, sometimes (when kinship is patrilineal and consequently more male-centered) as a balance to kinship groups also in the center (Maybury-Lewis forthcoming).

East African. Among several pastoral groups in East Africa, the formal age organization is also a channel for avoidance or management of conflict stemming from the parent-child knots in the rope of generational succession. The Arusha (Tanzania) value land as their most precious resource; they consequently keep land conflicts, which are typically across generations within a kin group, out of the "parish" assemblies of the age organization. In the arena of the age organization, which links the entire community, competition between adjacent generations is constrained. For the Samburu (Kenya), the scarcest prize is women, and polygamy places fathers and sons in direct competition for wives. In the Samburu age organization, authority over a man's sons is shifted into others' hands: he cannot be a powerful "firestick elder" to his own son. The Masai (Kenya and Tanzania) also prize women, and competition over women heightens family strife. When a first son enters the Masai warrior grade, his mother and her other sons move with him into a separate warrior village. Fathers and adult sons are distanced both spatially and by a formalization of relations across age lines (Spencer 1976). Words such as *formal* or *distant* should be understood in the structural sense. On a personal level, the rules and rituals of an age organization may make relations between a specific father and son less difficult.

Western Retirement Communities

In Chapter 3, Samburu warriors were compared to students in boarding schools and colleges because they are all subject to a moratorium on adulthood. Old people in separate retirement residences are in a latter-day set-aside situation, and vulnerable to exactly the same infuriating commentary from the powerful in the middle that "these should be the best years of your lives." The age-homogeneous residence for old people may also parallel the traditional age organizations as a tension deflector. Disagreements about norms and life-styles can be battled in a more formal and collective way between residents and directors, or between tenants' councils and representatives of HUD. Spatial separation also provides insulation from the abrasiveness of daily rubbing elbows with family members, whose tastes may be very different. Rules about noise, dress, and use of recreational facilities are less likely to be a source of conflict if they are imposed by the collectivity of older people on all young visitors. Financial arrangements between the generations for shelter, food, and care are also formalized between strangers, protecting a more voluntary and less instrumental atmosphere for the intimate intergenerational relations of the family.

Theoretical Implications of the Data

Whenever well-qualified observers offer opposing interpretations of a set of circumstances, it is possible that additional variables are intervening between the two major concepts under consideration. For example, intervening variables that might shape the relationship between separate residence and age conflict include duration of the residential separation, its inclusiveness (everyone in population, or certain groups only), extent of separateness (NB high involvement with children by members of old-age communities), stage of life at which separation occurs, and evaluation of the age border from both sides.

Definitional differences are another possible explanation for this kind of disagreement. In this case, the tendency to identify age ideology with age conflict may be part of the problem. It does seem highly likely that ideological orientations to age will be associated with spatial separation of age-groups. However, ideologies of age do not necessarily imply conflict. Among the Nyakyusa, for example, the values of "good company" and loyalty to an age-group are shared by everyone in the society. There are also many cross-cutting ties across the age boundaries, such as kinship, and the spatial separation itself does not involve great distances. The younger boys see their mothers every day, as the mothers take turns providing the meals the age-mates eat together.

Many years ago Emile Durkheim, a founder of modern sociology and anthropology, pointed out that there are two basic kinds of social bonds, and that one may lead to the other. *Mechanical solidarity* is a tie based on similarity, and many traditional societies are held together by this kind of glue. *Organic solidarity* is based on complementarity; individuals are tied to each other by their differences. Durkheim saw that in complex societies individuals might be most tightly woven into the social fabric through membership in mechanical groups, such as occupational organizations, which would be in turn linked together in organic complementarity (1933). Viewed in this framework, spatial separation of ages or other explicit recognition of age boundaries could be seen as conducive to mechanical solidarity within the age category, which in turn provides a basis for complementary integration—rather than conflict—with other ages. The case of old-age communities in modern society at least supports this as a possibility, because the individuals involved were often more socially marginal in "normal" neighborhoods than in these new settings. The inclusion of tenants' council officers from public housing for the elderly in meetings with other civic leaders is a small example of these movements in the direction of an organic integration with other generations (Hochschild 1973).

The content of an age ideology could, of course, also be antiagist. As we saw in Chapter 3, age is likely to become irrelevant within an age-homogeneous community recruited from an out-of-power age category. That age irrelevance, and the feelings of social self-sufficiency often engendered in these communities, may become the basis of an ideology that age should be less relevant in the wider society. In this case there might be an ideological conflict, but not exactly of one age-group against another. The conflict would instead be over the appropriateness of age boundaries at all.

"In the Eye of the Beholder": Assumptions and Expectations

In a version of the self-fulfilling prophecy, an important factor in how individuals who share some social characteristics view themselves is the way they believe others to see them. The concept of self-fulfilling prophecy refers to the social force of expectations. Students in a research lab who were told that their rats were especially smart animals found in their experiments that the rats performed exceptionally well—far better than identical rats whose trainers were not told to expect unusual intelligence. The same effect of expectations has been observed with trainers of humans: teachers who are told their students are unusually talented or the opposite tend to observe the predicted results, even when the students are the same in actual abilities. The point is that the way we expect people to behave has effects on how we treat them, and consequently on how they respond.

The most basic expectation or "prophecy" about individuals with some shared characteristics is that they are alike in some significant way. Persistent external recognition of the category as a meaningful collectivity is likely to elicit some kind of collective response, although that response may be to *deny* the validity of the collective identification. From this point of view, external recognition of old age as a significant social border in the United States has increased steadily since the 1920s. In the last sixty years, older people have been increasingly exposed to the expectation that their common age makes them a significant social collectivity. There are many indicators of these views from outside the age border: legislation concerning old people, research designs addressing old age, mass media programming about and for old people, specialized publications for the retired, and labels for the old as a social category.

Legislation

There has been a gradual progression in both legislation and research from viewing the old as a subset of some other social category, such as poor people, to a significant category in their own right, but still a problematic and hopefully temporary one, to final recognition of old people as a permanent and positive constituent of the society. The first legislative responses to old people included them in a broader category of poor people who needed financial assistance.

In 1935, the Social Security Act recognized age as a major basis for eligibility, but in combination with productivity. People did not receive government funds solely on the basis of age, but because they had worked and contributed to the system for a certain number of years. More recently, funds from the general treasury have been added to Social Security, reinforcing age on its own as the significant social boundary around eligible recipients. The creation of Supplemental Security Income continues this trend.

From the beginning of the Social Security program, there has been strong resistance to defining it as support from society for individuals in a certain age category. Although that now is clearly the case, both because of demographic shifts that require fewer workers to support more retired people, and because of payments into the fund out of general revenues, there is still reluctance to acknowledge that Social Security is not a piggy bank storing up workers' savings to be used by them in their old age. Public debate about the soundness of the so-called "insurance" plan, however, is making the actuality more and more clear. Resistance to acknowledgement of the age boundary as justification for social support comes from the negative attitudes of many Americans both toward "socialized" government policies and toward explicit acknowledgement of social differentiation of any kind. In spite of this resistance, however, both the facts of the system and awareness of them have sharpened a social boundary around older people.

A continuing theme in the history of financial legislation concerning old people has been the notion that if their common problems, such as low income, were removed, they might blend back into the general population and lose their distinctiveness as a social category. If old people are distinctive only by virtue of their common problems, the logic goes, if the problems are removed they should lose their distinctiveness. This assumption overlooks both the self-fulfilling prophecy consequences of treating old people as a category *during* the social problem-solving phase and also the possibility that they might have *positive* things in common.

The various problems are gradually being pried apart from the idea of old people as a social category. The emerging recognition that the old-age category will continue to exist even after the problems are solved is embodied most clearly in legislative terms by the creation in the 1960s of a separate Administration on Aging. Although AOA focuses primarily on the problems of older people, its existence is also a structural acknowledgement of the old as a distinct and permanent constituency. Even the debates over abolishment of mandatory retirement, which can be seen as explicit arguments about the appropriateness of an age border, are focusing attention on age. As I suggested in Chapter 1, abolishment of mandatory retirement would not likely remove the age boundary, but rather redefine its markers as functional rather than chronological. It is to be hoped that the positive progression will continue on to attempts to encourage more participation of old people in the society, more use of what they have to offer to balance concerns about what to do *for* them.

Research

An anthropological specialty called ethnoscience emphasizes that more understanding of a culture may come from discovery of what questions it considers salient and reasonable than from collecting data to answer questions brought in by investigators. Research designs are one indicator of the questions our society has considered important on the topic of aging. Through the years, there has been a shift parallel to that in the legislative domain from a view of the age border as problematic and temporary to assumptions that it may persist, and even have positive aspects.

The earliest research on old age asked questions about how to cure its physical ills. The next step was to search for solutions to its social problems. The early issues of journals and agendas of meetings are a litany of age-related ills affecting first the physical, then the social body. The underlying assumption in all this earlier work is that the distinctiveness of the old as a category is derived from their common problems: when the problems were solved, therefore, the category should disappear.

As researchers began to listen to the answers to their own questions, however, the picture began to change. Most old people did not have the physical and social problems they were supposed to: they were not as sick or as isolated as researchers expected them to be, and they did not all want to live with their children, or to spend all their time being grandparents. The most recent shift in research on age is away from what we need to do *for* old people, or how they get along with us, to their own views of age, the structure of their daily lives, and the supports that they offer each other. Behind the newest questions is the notion that what old people know and do and create in this new stage of the human life has a positive contribution to make to the rest of society. At the same time that research results repeatedly reveal the diversity of individual responses to the old-age grade as a distinctive segment of the life course, the structural embodiment of this recognition in the research domain is the creation, in 1974, of the National Institute on Aging.

The Media

An intrinsically American indicator of existence as a social category is to be treated as such by the media, especially television. Programming is directed at various segments of our population, now including the "older adult." Nationwide broadcasts like *Over Easy,* from KQED in San Francisco, signal and stimulate awareness of an age boundary. Viewers identifying themselves as older Americans are tuning in the show, and the messages it sends out are both practical and positive acknowledgements of the needs and potentials distinctive to this age-grade. The contrast with the damning praise of the "extraordinary" oldsters used in the 1950s to demonstrate that

Life Begins at Eighty is striking. On that show, old people were praised, in a rather patronizing style, for the feat of remaining alive socially as well as physically for so long. *Over Easy* assumes that its audience is alert and active and offers examples and advice to help enhance the quality of their lives. Housing alternatives, small-portion recipes, and fitness are typical features.

Specialized publications such as *Modern Maturity* and *Harvest Years* are also aimed at an older audience. Finally, an acknowledgement of old age as a persistent category in our society is the linguistic flurry of labels for it. Senior citizens, mature Americans, and elders are all new dramatis personae. A recent national survey shows the extent to which the appropriateness of a label has been accepted. "Senior citizen" is the most popular label among Americans over sixty-five. The more significant statistic is that 83 percent chose some label at all (NCOA 1976).

The Old Themselves

One contemporary gerontologist sums up the effect of all these different approaches to the age border as an atmosphere of salience for age (Cutler 1981). Certainly the root cause of this salience is the increasing number of old people in our population; the responses of legislators, researchers, and television programmers to that increase are the vehicles through which the numbers take on social meaning. The consequence of these various forms of external recognition for the age border should be development of age ideologies among the old themselves.

As Mannheim observed, there may be several generation units—or ideologies—among members of one age stratum. Even if age peers have in common an ideological response to age, the content of these responses may not be the same. There are several age ideologies among older Americans. In parallel to the external attitudes, the earliest political action by older people was aimed at solving problems, such as low income. Later came integrationist style ideologies, with an opposite approach: the stress was on the similarity of most old people to everyone else, in justification for demands to end discrimination on the basis of age in various domains. Another ideological response is emphasis of the age boundary in movements that claim old people are a distinct category, and furthermore have positive contributions to make to the society at large.

The various political organizations of old people that promote these different ideologies are discussed in detail in Chapter 6. The point here is that the external recognition of an old age category in America in the last sixty years has, in fact, elicited ideological responses. The aura of age salience Cutler identifies is, in addition, likely to intensify the significance of age identity for future old people, who will have grown old in this atmosphere.

Age Ideology and the Individual

Although it is possible to talk about the existence of ideology and the factors that may encourage it on a social level, that ideology is an aggregate of individual responses. There is very little evidence, however, about the causes of ideological responses to age on the individual level. Two clearly stated hypotheses about ideological salience of age are available, but at first inspection appear to be contradictory. On the one hand, Rose suggests that old people with higher class positions and more resources will be the most likely "to retain more contact with the larger society . . . and hence acquire less of a distinctive aging subculture" (1968, p. 30). On the other hand, Trela argues that the greater the inconsistency between an old person's statuses, the more likely he or she will be to respond to age-oriented political appeals (1976). Since inconsistencies between ascribed and achieved statuses are especially stressful, the old people most likely to feel part of an age collectivity with common political interests should be those whose achieved statuses are highest, and therefore most inconsistent with the low ascriptive position of old age.

There are several intervening factors that may resolve this apparent contradiction. First of all, as we saw in Chapter 2, old people of higher class positions are more resistant to identifying themselves as old, which would support Rose. Once they do make that identification, however, they should be more active in pursuing their political interest, according to general research on the relationship between class and political participation—which offers some support for Trela. Also, not all age ideologies are identical. For example, old people from more privileged backgrounds may develop political attitudes based on a desire to protect resources that will permit avoidance of an age-group identification. Another important point is Rose's assumption that contact with the younger society will reduce the likelihood of age ideology. This may not be the case. If younger people hold stereotypes about old age—as we have seen some do— then *more* contact with them might arouse ideological reactions among the old people who reject the stereotypes.

The significance of age boundaries is not necessarily constant. It may vary, for instance, according to the type of issue on a public agenda. Material issues, according to Foner, are least likely to stimulate alignments along the age border; ideal issues are the most likely to have that result. She suggests that material issues tend to reflect class interests that cross-cut age lines, and are also more easily compromised than less tangible bones of contention. The inevitability of aging should also reduce age division over economic issues, since younger people have hopes of benefitting in the future from advantages given to the old. Economic benefits for old people may also affect their families, so that the rewards are spread across age lines even in the short-run. Finally, Foner argues that ideal issues may lead to feelings that basic political changes are required to resolve the problems, and this is the kind of change that older people are most likely to oppose because of their greater "conservative" attachment to the overall structure of their society (1972, pp. 152–54). Cross-cultural evidence provides some support for Foner, and also raises some questions. Among the Abron of Gyaman, Terray found that intergenerational conflicts were reduced by the younger people's anticipation of taking over the elders' power and resources (1975). The caveat is that such anticipation is not likely to be universal. In fact, as I suggested in Chapter 1, Americans seem extraordinarily capable of denying their own future role as old people.

Conclusion

Like the ideologies that they seek to explain, the many hypotheses about factors promoting age ideology must be tested out in the real world. The various views from different cultural contexts, and focused on different levels of human activity, add up to a strong suggestion that age ideologies will continue to ferment around the old-age boundary in the United States. In the next chapter, we will observe how old people "vote with their feet" on the issue of age differentiation and examine the conditions under which age peers become important members of the informal social networks that define the interactional dimension of an age border.

Chapter

5

Age
and Informal
Interaction

Old people's social contacts with each other provide a *behavioral* map of age categorization. This behavioral and informal significance of age-mates may be quite distinct from formally organized groups, or from normative rules about what roles age-mates ought to or are desired to play. The clearest fact about the significance of age in the informal social lives of old people anywhere is that we know next to nothing about it. As in many other areas of inquiry, the formal and the normative have received more attention—they're easier to find—than the informal. What is known about informal ties is mainly quantitative, although we have little understanding of what we are counting. Yet creation and maintenance of roles for the elderly in industrial society must initially be rooted in the informal sphere (see Rosow 1976, p. 479), and much policy discussion concerns reinforcement of "natural support networks." The best information we have is about residents of special settings such as retirement communities—again, they're easier to find. The benefits to these people of peer ties to these individuals are so clear, however, and the trade-off costs so low, that what we do know about them is a strong stimulus to learning more about the role of age-mates in the lives of old people in more ordinary circumstances. In this chapter we will retrace the steps of the anthropologists who have investigated peer ties among old people, beginning with community studies of special settings, and then moving out into the wider world to hypothesize about the conditions and consequences of age-ties for old people in general.

Community Studies

The earliest firsthand research by anthropologists on old age was done in age-homogeneous communities (see Ross 1977; Fry 1979; Byrne 1971; Hendel-Sebestyen 1979). The broadest question behind these studies is whether age could provide a foundation for community; the consistent answer is yes. In mobile-home parks, highrise public housing, luxury condominiums, union and church sponsored residences, in the United States, France, and England, these ethnographers found both the emotional and the structural aspects of community. The old people studied feel they are part of a collectivity, that their destinies are woven together with those of other residents; and the routines of their daily lives trace the regular patterns of interaction that define social organization. Most of these patterns develop and exist outside of, or even in opposition to, more formal organization imposed by community managers or administrators (see Keith 1980b for a review of community creation in age-homogeneous settings).

The superficial characteristics of the various settings in which old people have formed communities are, at least to an anthropologist's eye, delightfully diverse. In the French residence, wine bottles appear on tables, food is a major focus of recreation, and factions line up along political cleavages. In Florida, old black men go fishing in a pond while Cuban women exchange gossip across balcony railings; in California, working class women quilt, crochet, and align themselves by Baptist church affiliations, while in a middle-class condominium, couples play bridge, golf, and gather in cocktail party cliques. However, the most important aspect of cultural diversity in these peer communities may be its superficiality.

Below the surface differences in style, and even language, are significant similarities. First of all, social organization exists, and level of social activity is high. The fact that older people among themselves create full, patterned, active social lives deserves mention only because of the view taken by many younger people that complete lives for the old must be centered on *us*. These social lives are functional as well as fun. The extensive aid available from peers allows many older residents to be secure without giving up independence: acceptance of help from a peer does not connote dependence in the way that support from a child or an institution might. The giver of help also acquires a precious superiority in what one observer has labelled the "hierarchy of poor dears" (Hochschild 1973).

Second, the social organizations created in old-age communities are distinctive from the outside worlds in which they are embedded. As we saw in the discussion of norms, responses to death and to sex are distilled into normative patterns markedly different in some ways from those outside. As morale is higher in age-homogeneous contexts even for members without high social participation, the existence of such shared norms seems to be the key feature linking age-homogeneity to morale. In addition, the emphasis on equality sharply differentiates the status ranking systems inside old people's communities from those outside them. As among the warriors of East African age-graded societies, ranking in terms of skills or activities exercised in the present, and particularly identified with the group, is more acceptable than ranking based in the past, or on external scales: being a good shot is an appropriate basis of status among warriors, being a good shuffleboard player, or an elected official inside the community is an appropriate basis of status in a retirement community. The significance of age itself is an excellent indicator of this distinctiveness in ranking. Age is typically irrelevant to rank inside an age-homogeneous community—although that perceived homogeneity may include a thirty-year span of chronological age (Ross 1977, pp. 66–84).

Other basic characteristics also take on different meaning inside old-age communities. Sex roles are often less distinct, and in some cases, although men and women participate in the communities differently, those differences are indicated in new ways. Ethnicity is a less imposing social border inside several multiracial United States age communities than in the society outside (Kandel and Heider 1979; Wellin and Boyer 1979). In the French residence where I lived, politics was imported from the outside as the most significant social identity, but put to distinctive use inside, as Catholic holidays became Communist celebrations, and each leisure activity acquired a factional identity. Ethnically homogeneous communities display a similar "recycling" of cultural raw materials. Jewish old people in a Venice, California, Senior Citizens Center remain very Jewish, but in adaptation to the demands and restrictions of a new situation, rituals and symbols are created and modified out of the basic raw materials of Eastern European Jewish culture. One old man celebrated his own birth-death day by finishing his speech, with the help of an oxygen mask, before the "angel of death" arrived. The man's will included a bequest to the Center to make possible a new ritual—celebration of his birthday for five more years, until he would have been one hundred. The Sabbath at the Center begins well before sundown, so that the old people can come and go safely in the dangerous neighborhood (Myerhoff 1978). The expression and use of Jewishness at the Aliyah Center is as different from that outside it as the significance of Communism at Les Floralies is different from that in Paris at large.

Another reprise of the "old people are people" theme is the importance of conflict in these communities. Fighting is an activity we seldom associate with the old. Most people who worried about

This resident of a French retirement residence told me, "I hadn't played cards for twenty-five years before I moved in; now I play every day." Age-homogeneous groups offer opportunities for increased social participation to many old people in modern, industrial societies. (Photo by Jennie Keith)

the boredom and depression I would surely face as a young member of an old-age community shared an image of old people as peaceable to the point of stagnation. As in any other community ever observed, communities of old people are scenes of battle as well as of cohesiveness. Whether factional allegiances are to Baptist churches or to political *tendances,* they are present, and can erupt into intense conflict. I was almost thrown out of Les Floralies for my alleged part in a complex election fight involving secret slates, clandestine meetings, accusations of corruption, attempts to influence senile voters, and ultimate insults impugning candidates' characters on the basis of their activities during the World War II Resistance. Difficult as such factional machinations may make life for administrators, it is a sign of life from the old people who care enough for their community to fight about it.

Why so much conflict in old-age communities? Not because they are old people, but because they are new communities. In communities formed unintentionally, that is without a shared goal or ideology to define and launch them, conflict is likely to develop over what the definition of the emerging community should be. The likelihood of conflict increases with the lack of alternative options open to its members, and their consequent commitment to the one at hand. Like it or not, residents of many old-age communities perceive few alternatives, and assume that they will live out their lives there.

The essential finding about communities of old people is that they exist. This raises two questions: Why? and So what? To discover why, the first step is to compare cases and discover what they have in common. Here the answer is clear: they all have at least 50 percent old people. The variation in every other aspect of their settings, cultures, and formal organization puts great emphasis on their age-homogeneity as the key factor. What these communities seem to teach us is that when old people have access to their peers, they "take advantage of them" to create norms and behavior patterns that increase their well-being. That is, of course, the answer to "so what?" The people in old-age communities, compared to those in mixed-age settings, appear to have higher morale, greater opportunity for social participation, and greater access to tangible support when they need it. Interpretation of the studies that show these results is, however, difficult (cf Carp 1976). They may compare people who moved into subsidized housing with those who did not, and better housing may have a lot to do with their good feelings about themselves and their lives. Those who move into resort areas may be divided into those who enter age-homogeneous communities and those who do not: those in the retirement communities have higher morale, but the entire category of those who move across state lines is a statistical minority. Residents of HUD-subsidized housing may be compared in terms of whether they live in age-mixed or elderly projects; however, other differences among residents in age-mixed housing, such as class and/or ethnicity, may confound the results.

Where should the community studies lead us, then? Back out

Women peeling vegetables as payment for their room and board in a Buddhist old-age home (Hong Kong) are a reminder that the ideals of filial piety and support for aging parents may not be realized for all. (Photo by Charlotte Ikels)

into the surrounding society. The levels of community, and their benefits, are striking enough to spur investigation to unravel the inconclusive evidence. To do this, the focus must be on age bonds themselves, viewed as distinctly as possible from type of housing, moving, and social attributes other than age. Will older people *outside* special settings use age-mates when they are available to create norms and social networks? If they do, will the material and emotional benefits observed in the old-age communities result?

Age Bonds Outside of Communities

Direct evidence for the most straightforward source of age ties does exist outside of special communities: the availability of peers in the immediate residential area does stimulate actual contact with those peers. When "density" of age-mates in apartment buildings reaches 50 percent or more, for instance, the number of local friends increases (Rosow 1967). (The 50 percent "tipping point" is the same as in some of the formal communities, such as IdleHaven, where older people are only about half the population (Johnson 1971). Even outside the residential concentration of apartment buildings, the proportion of older people in a neighborhood affects the likelihood that older people's friends will also be old (Rosenberg 1970).

In case the availability-actuality relationship of old neighbors to old friends seems obvious, it must be remembered that proximity does *not* promote social closeness *across* age lines. Older people in more than one age-integrated setting have trekked across courtyards or upstairs to seek out other old people, rather than visiting the young neighbors placed next door by the social engineers (Rosenmayr and Köckeis 1962; Alger 1959). Old people, by choosing other old people as friends are, of course, acting just like young people.

In friendship choices, as in every other way, old people are diverse. Although general patterns of age homophily, facilitated by proximity, exist, there are individual attributes that increase "sensitivity" to age density. In the Cleveland apartment buildings, for instance, women, people over seventy-five, and those who had experienced more extensive role losses, were more influenced in their friendship choices by availability of other old people; and age density had a stronger effect on members of the working class than on those in the middle class (Rosow 1967).

The consequences of these age ties are apparently as beneficial outside as inside residential communities. Age density in the Cleveland apartments was positively related both to the use of neighbors as role models—increasing potential for definition of age norms—and to decreased anxiety about illness because neighbors became an important source of support. Similar findings appear in Philadelphia, where older people with active friendship networks have less need for support services, regardless of their actual physical health (Moss, Gottesman, and Kleban 1976).

Knowing that age ties do exist when peers are available, that there is individual variation in response to that availability, and that peer ties have obvious benefits, the stage is set for a more thorough investigation of the conditions under which peers become important in older people's social networks, and the consequences of such informal age boundaries for the quality of their lives. Two sources of guidance are available for these explorations: general social theories about affiliation, which have not yet been thoroughly applied to age; and cross-cultural data about age differentiation, which have not yet been "brought home" for integration into gerontological research.

Conditions of Informal Age Bonds: The Social Level

Homophily

The general principle of homophily is intensified under two kinds of stress, one produced by lack of social definition, the other by what might be called overdefinition. Ambiguity is a painful aspect of new roles, which some individuals must define for themselves because their society has outlined a form but not yet filled in any content. Conflicting expectations of various role partners may also create ambiguities about priorities of response. Or the transition from one social role to another may strand individuals in a temporarily ambiguous status "betwixt and between." Older people are likely to experience all of these ambiguities, and with fewer of the social supports provided at earlier life stages. Since order and definition are a basic aspect of any human way of life, it is no exaggeration to call social ambiguity an inhuman stress. Others who have suffered in similar circumstances have found, logically enough, that the best assistance came from fellow sufferers. Since reduction of social ambiguity requires collective resolution, the most likely collectivity to turn to is composed of those with both the understanding and the motivation required.

New Roles

Divorced single parent is an example of a new role in American society, the lack of a positive definition for which has promoted bonds of friendship and mutual support distilled in some cases into formal organizations, such as Parents Without Partners. In the casual context of picnics or parties these role pioneers are also about the serious business of filling in norms of appropriate behavior for this newly numerous category. The school superintendent is a classic victim of role conflict, bombarded with irreconcilable expectations from various sets of role partners including teachers, parents, students, and fellow superintendents. Occupants of this strained role tend to socialize intensively among themselves (Gross, Mason, and McEachern 1957). This peer contact offers blessed relief from conflicting demands, but in addition provides an opportunity for mutual development of strategies for managing the role's built-in ambiguities.

One of the first official social science labels applied to old age was "roleless role" (Burgess 1950). Since it is new in the history of the human species to have an extended stage of life between work and death, the people Neugarten calls the "young-old" face a roleless role with a vengeance. Like school superintendents or divorcees, old people are people, but in this case, pioneering people in a profound sense. If new roles, with their ambiguity of norms and expectations, promote ties to peers, then older people should be even more likely to develop peer ties than others faced with undefined roles in a shallower sense. Given the stigma of old age in some modern societies, however, the comfort of peers may not be worth the price of public association with them. Old age is not really without definition, since it does have a negative valence. Ironically, what unhelpful social definition of age that does exist may be an impressive obstacle to peer creation of definitions positive and specific enough to provide guidance for a new life-stage.

The research required to discover the relationship between stigma and peer ties may be difficult to do because of the stigma itself. Even those peer ties that do exist may not be accurately reported. An older person who suspects the questioner of negative views toward the aged, or who shares many of those views, may minimize how many and how important are his or her ties to other old people. The tremendous emotional significance of family bonds leads to their being emphasized when people report about their social lives. That qualitative significance is, of course, crucial information, but it should not obscure the actual contact and support shared with peers. The only way to be sure of getting both kinds of data is to put in the hours of observation rather than relying only on reports (Keith 1980c).

An excellent example of the rewards in accuracy and insight that may come from combining extended observation with interview report is anthropological research in single room occupancy hotels. The residents of these hotels are characterized by ferocious independence; their view of themselves as loners is probably their most precious possession. Asked direct questions about friendship ties or social support, they typically deny any. The only ties they do acknowledge are those with family. Anthropologists who have lived and worked in SROs, however, have learned that it is peer networks that make possible maintenance of the prized loner image. Once they knew about the existence of these networks, the researchers could interview residents with specific questions about personnel, location, and function of specific network links. "You can't be a loner on your own" is an appropriate summary of these studies. Detailed "network profiles" reveal frequent and diverse social supports—hours of informal visiting, loans, shared food, help in emergencies, emotional unburdening, shared advice. This research has two kinds of significance: it adds more data to demonstrate the tendency toward peer grouping among the old; and it waves a warning flag against any attempt to study social networks without extensive observation of actual behavior (Cohen and Sokolovsky 1980; Sokolovsky and Cohen 1978, 1981).

We have learned as much as we know about residents of old-age communities by moving in on them. To have the same extensive and qualitative understanding of the informal social lives of the majority of old people who do not live in these special settings, we need to come as close to moving in as possible. "Ethnographies of age" must also be done in the natural communities where most old people live,

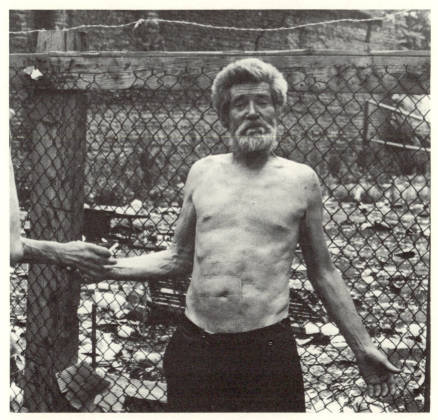

Residents of SRO hotels are often life-long loners who create networks of support among themselves to avoid intimacy or dependence entailed by help from others (New York City). (Photo by Jay Sokolovsky)

the footwork put in to follow out their social networks, and the listening hours accumulated to hear their perceptions and evaluations of life in old age.

Liminality

Liminality derives from the Latin word for threshold: it refers to a phase of transition from one social state to another. Couples on their honeymoon, recruits entering boot camp, pilgrims en route from profane to sacred space, initiates suspended between nonmembership and belonging are all in liminal states. Liminality is not only between more structured states of existence, it is also an antithesis of normal structure. Most normal roles are "neutralized" in liminal periods. If hair styles represent social position, then initiands' heads are shaved. If speech usually indicates status relations, then verbal control is abolished and obscenity prevails. Special secret argots are often acquired and used during liminal experiences (see Legesse 1973b, p. 115).

Individuals in liminal states are often perceived as temporarily not quite human—either more than human, i.e., sacred, or less than human, i.e., animalistic or not yet cultured enough to be fully human. As representative of the antithesis of what is fully ordered human social life in a particular setting, liminal individuals and experiences clarify by contrast the appropriate structures of ordinary life. This contrast is itself a structured opposition, and liminality is not without its own rules. If heads are to be shaved in antithesis to status marking hairstyles, then initiands do not have the choice of shaving or not shaving. If everyone at a personal growth seminar is supposed to strip in liberation from status-marking dress, then no one is free to keep clothes on.

Rituals of passage such as marriages or initiations provide roadmaps across the cultural no-man's land of liminality. The rite of passage itself is subdivided into a metaphor of the transition it both guides and represents: each ritual is composed of three stages—separation, marginality, and reincorporation. The marginal, or liminal, stage is a fallow field for communality and creativity, as it offers temporary respite from status differentiation and normative structures (Turner 1969). Learning with and from peers is a central aspect of many of these rituals. One particular characteristic of roles recruited by age is that they must be relearned repeatedly (Legesse 1979). Unlike other social identities, age-roles by definition cannot be learned once and for all, as each age-linked stage requires resocialization.

Individuals who share experiences of the liminal often share feelings of *communitas,* unstructured, spontaneous, communal feeling. One of the poignant aspects of liminal experience is the difficulty of carrying these intense and diffuse feelings back out into the every day world. The logical and empirical link between liminality and age peers is that the "social clocks" of many cultures move age-mates through liminal stages together, so the egalitarian potentialities of age are accentuated in the combination of celebration and ordeal typical of most rites of passage. Liminality both evokes and is eased by solidarity with others in the same circumstances, and age-mates often experience liminal stages together.

Old people in industrial societies are, however, stranded in the liminal: exit signs are clearly marked, but reincorporation is not on the map. Their choice is between cultural bushwhacking and clinging to the crumbling cliff of midlife roles. If liminality offers an opportunity for creativity, then older people in modern societies face opportunity on a fearful scale. As at other ages and in other cultures, creativity is most likely in the company of peers. Entire life-stages are defined as liminal in some other cultures; among the Boran of Kenya, the first and the last generation grades are liminal (Legesse 1973b, p. 115). However, both the boundaries and the content of these temporarily marginal and sacred statuses are clearly specified and transient antistructure, rather than the permanent nonstructure surrounding the old in modern contexts.

Residents of old-age communities invent rites of passage and create the norms and roles that offer an end stage for the ritual to move toward. The move into an age-homogeneous community is itself a rite of passage; and, in addition, the specific patterns of socialization into many old-age communities follow the three-stage formula. At Les Floralies, for example, finding a permanent seat in the dining room was both the means and the metaphor for social incorporation (Ross, Keith, 1977, ch. 6). The broader question is whether liminality is a stimulus to peer bonding and mutual socialization outside separate residential settings. Strong hints in the yes direction come from the evidence that role loss makes individuals more "sensitive" to age density (Rosow 1967). Widowhood in the United States is a poignant example of role exit into liminality without clear routes to reentry. The presence of other widows in the neighborhood does ease adjustment, through actual support as well as through reference groups which assist in the definition of new roles (see Blau 1961).

Asked in a symposium on *The Elderly of the Future* to make predictions from my perspective as an anthropologist, my first answer was that I forsaw a great deal of work for cross-cultural researchers. No topic is a better example than liminality of the amount of future work required to understand the social significance of age. If informal aspects of old-age sociability are little studied, then its liminal aspects—the antithesis of formal social organization—are, not surprisingly, understood least of all. Thorough understanding of liminality as a possible stimulus to informal peer ties will require several kinds of comparison. On a societal level, cultures in which older people categorically are and are not placed in liminal phases can be compared. Comparison must also focus—both within and among cultures—on variation in the collectivity of liminal experiences associated with age. In addition, individuals should be compared in terms of their perceived experiences of liminality to determine whether they define certain points in their lives as transitional, and whether they see those phases as associated with age, as idiosyncratic or shared with others, and whether those others are primarily identified as age-mates. All of the information about age-linked transitions must then be connected to fully charted networks of social interaction.

Stereotypes and Stigma

Social contact among people with some characteristics in common may also be stimulated by the opposite of ambiguity; certain kinds of external overdefinition may also push people together. Stereotyping and stigma by outsiders may make other victims of these negative overgeneralizations a blessed refuge. The double jeopardy here is that associating with other old people may reinforce some of the stereotypes, and perpetuate some of the stigma, from which peer ties offer temporary relief (Goffman 1963; Ross 1975). It seems most likely that older individuals who find negative responses the most shocking—that is those who have enjoyed higher statuses throughout their lives—are the most reluctant to seek comfort whose price is visible association with similarly disvalued peers. Residential density of peers, for instance, has a stronger effect on the sociability of working class than middle class old people (Rosow 1967). Part of this difference is explained by the greater tendency of working class individuals to find their friends close to home, but the status discrepancy hypothesis may account for some difference too.

Threat

The extreme edge of overrecognition from outsiders is threat. Studies of community formation in many contexts—nation-states, utopias, squatters—show that a moderate level of threat from an identifiable source is a stimulus to communal feeling and organization. Comparison of the old-age communities rings in the "old people are people" theme again, as threat also appears as a source of community formation among them. Security is a major reason that old people choose to live in any age-homogeneous residential environment. This is partly provided by the closed areas and policing offered by organized communities, but it comes also from the absence of younger people who are seen as more dangerous than peers. In addition, inside age-homogeneous residences, old people such as the retired construction workers of Les Floralies, discover that they share fears of financial insecurity based on mistrust of the motives or judgment of younger directors or developers (see also Fry 1979).

Whether perceived threat might promote peer networks outside of separate residential settings is not known, but plausible enough to be worth investigation. The old people who dance and pray together at the Aliyah Senior Center described by Myerhoff are, for example, painfully aware of the dangers in the streets and alleys surrounding it. The warmth and humanity inside the Center's walls bind its members even closer because of the contrasting cold world outside. Even the timing of Sabbath is redefined in the Aliyah world to preserve it as a haven from after-dark dangers. Certainly older people with peer supports—even outside of organized communities—do feel more secure (see also Moss 1976; Rosow 1967). The beneficial consequence argues for exploration of triggering conditions.

Cross-Cutting Ties

Age similarity, combined with other homogeneities, does promote informal ties. What happens when age is cross-cut, rather than paralleled by other social identities or allegiances? Raising this question is a reminder to restate the basic but productive principle that age bonds are most likely to develop when few cross-cutting ties are present. The explanatory productivity of this principle comes from its leading us to look for stages of the life course, cultural contexts, or social situations in which age has least "competition." Some anthropologists have even suggested that age has a residual quality, that it is *only* a significant principle in society when few others are available (Schurtz 1902; Needham 1974). A look across cultures, and down the life span, however, suggests that age often performs a more complicated balancing act of complementarity with other attributes.

In terms of times and places when age has little competition as a basis of social bonding, adolescence and old age are, in many cultures, the life stages with fewest types of social linkage; age-mates and kin predominate. Intense peer ties among adolescents are stimulated by shared liminality, as well as by the classic ambiguities of a search for self-identity. It is also true that age-mates win partly by default, since in many social settings adolescents have not yet acquired the adult roles of work, parenthood, politics, religion, and so on, that would compete with age. One reason that the old gang fades into reminiscence is that its former members are too busy and divided by too many loyalties to maintain it (e.g., Whyte 1955). However, we are less accustomed to thinking about the fact that a new gang may be formed or the old one revived *after* the roles of social maturity have receded.

In the culturally defined life careers of many societies, adolescence and old age are symmetrical transitions in and out of social maturity, with a parallel lack of competition for age ties at the same time that liminality and need for socialization make them attractive. In a rural Hungarian village, for instance, revival of the old gang is exactly what occurs. Adolescent peer group sociability fades during adult years, but is the basis for social contact and emotional support once again in old age (Fel and Hofer 1969, cited in Neugarten and Hagestad 1976, p. 42). Very little is known about such waxing and waning of peer ties in modern societies. There are enough tantalizing bits of evidence, however, to tempt researchers to a real feast. In the two classic studies of residential density and age bonds, the areas with greatest age density also had greatest residential stability, suggesting revival or maintenance rather than creation of age friendships (Rosow 1967; Rosenberg 1970). The age community studies show the possibility of reviving a pattern of peer ties, but with new personnel. A San Francisco survey found that the scores for "friendship participation" (number plus contact) declined through middleage, then rose in the sixties (Lowenthal, Thurner, and Chiriboga 1975, p. 51). The *meaning* of friendship appeared similar for adolescents and older people in another United States study which found that for both age categories friends were valued as sources of status definition (Gibbs-Candy 1976).

The task is to disentangle the individual experiences, community characteristics, and cultural expectations producing the various patterns. Are individuals with intense and satisfying peer group ties at adolescence, for example, most likely to revive them later, either with the same individuals or with others? One unexpected benefit to some deaf Americans is the lasting peer bonds created by attending special schools: these peer supports, intensified by a shared understanding of handicap and a shared communication system learned in a collective socialization experience, persist into old age (Becker 1980). Are residentially stable neighborhoods likely to promote peer ties, regardless of age density? Might age density combined with residential instability also promote peer groups of "new" older people precisely because they do not have deep roots in the community (see Fennell 1981)?

"Generation gap" has been a provocative tag for the relationships, or nonrelationships, of adolescents to their parents. The abrasive potential of relations between adjacent generations is another similarity between adolescents and older people: both have problems of role shift and authority with the generation in the middle. In cross-cultural view, alternate generation bonds appear when authority is vested in the middle-age category, the most common circumstance (Apple 1956). The conflictual rub of adjacent generations may also stimulate grouping among age peers. Among the Tiv of Northern Nigeria, for example, the adult men within a kin group control cattle which younger men need to obtain brides. Since in this polygynous society the older men would prefer to have additional wives themselves, there is a conflict of interest. Among the Tiv it is the young man's age-mates who bring a horizontal leverage through the age organization against the vertical pull of kinship. This pattern has been hypothesized to be general: when the kin group impedes the younger persons' access to social maturity, age grouping is likely to appear (Eisenstadt 1956).

An even broader pattern may be that when the household is not *adequate* to prepare the young for participation in the wider society, age-groups are likely to appear as an interstitial or interlinking sphere. Here the argument is abstract: if the principles guiding social relationships within the household are not those that predominate in the outside world, then a transition is necessary. Links among family members, who are usually the majority of residents in a household, are typically particularistic and ascribed—that is, guided by the sex, age, and kinship attributes of individuals, and focused on them as particular individuals rather than as members of a category. In some societies, where kinship is the type for social relation in every domain, norms of interaction acquired in the household may be extended appropriately beyond it, but societies in which universalistic and achieved principles predominate outside the household require a transition. Universalistic norms emphasize categorical rather than personal attributes. According to universalistic principles, people would be recruited to government jobs by scores on examinations, rather than by family connections. Achieved attributes are those acquired through life by individuals, in contrast to ascribed characteristics which are determined, usually permanently, at birth. Age groups, melding universalistic and ascriptive criteria, are, according to Eisenstadt, the perfect response. Extended schooling outside the home, for instance, is the setting for just the kind of transitional age grouping he predicts.

Stepping back to view the entire life course in many societies suggests again that there may be a structural parallel between adolescence and "young" old age. If one is the transition into and the other the transition out of social maturity, then perhaps Eisenstadt's argument about interlinking spheres could be extended to old age. The key question becomes, what is the transition into at the later stage? Is there the same asymmetry of structural principles to stimulate age-grouping? A shift toward more particularistic relationships would fulfill the conditions, and nothing is more particularistic than a family. Family ties do become more predominant, at least as sources of support for older members of many modern societies (Shanas et al. 1968; Shanas 1979). Although the concrete mapping of kinds and quality of social networks is not yet available to test Eisenstadt's abstract hypothesis, the hints we have make exploration look well worth the effort.

Conditions of Informal Age Bonds: The Individual Level

The "spreading fan" of personal development toward old age guarantees significant diversity in older people's informal socialization, as it does in other aspects of their lives. As the broad outlines of informal social networks are barely beginning to be charted, it is not surprising that the finer details of individual diversity have not been filled in. Two basic strategies for discovering this diversity are attention to the lifelong peer experiences of older individuals and documentation of their exposure to, and perceptions of, conditions that appear to promote peer ties more generally—experience of new roles or role losses, perceptions of threat, stigmatization or stereotyping, attitudes toward age, self-identification in age terms, sociability, and independence.

Longitudinal research on these, as on so many questions, is the ideal technique. Like other expensive and elusive ideals, however, it should encourage us to strive, rather than to give up and wait for absolute perfection. In the meantime, life histories are a cheaper and far simpler alternative that will produce sensitive and abundant data. Surprisingly, life histories of older individuals in any cultural settings are rare. The life histories we do have do not reveal much about the interaction of a social context and normal aging because, from a scientific point of view, we do not know whose lives they are. Too often, an allegedly typical person speaks for an entire culture, or one notably atypical person relates one extraordinary life. In neither case are diversity or pattern in the aging experience revealed. Life histories, like other avenues to qualitative data, increase in scientific value proportionately to the quality of the sampling procedure for choosing the individuals whose stories will be told (see Frank 1980 on life history, Keith 1980c on sampling in qualitative research).

Conditions of Informal Age Bonds: The Situational Level

Liminality is an attribute of situations which individuals may experience momentarily or over very long periods of time. Retirement and widowhood are followed by periods of liminality which may be experienced more or less collectively, and with more or less ritualized guidance from social norms. New groups of any kind are situations likely to present the social ambiguity that promotes focus on ascriptive characteristics, which are universally available and conveniently obvious. Ethnicity appears to be used as this kind of sorting filter in new African cities, for example (Mitchell 1956), and age, sex, and ethnicity in new college dormitories (Hess 1972). Older individuals who participate in new collectivities, residential or otherwise, would therefore be likely to be particularly influenced in the direction of age homophily.

Conclusion

Age symbolizes, evokes, and protects equality among peers. Peer ties should be most numerous and significant in informal social networks under conditions that promote an emphasis on equality. When the information available about peer ties is plotted in time and space, several patterns suggest when these conditions will be present. Peer ties develop as an egalitarian or horizontal balance to the vertical strain of hierarchy. Material as well as social needs may be met by peers in a spirit of reciprocity that does not require admission of dependence. A world of age-mates insulates from external ranking members of an age-grade temporarily or permanently excluded from power. The sometimes painful equality of shared status transitions also bonds peers together as colearners and coteachers. Shared experience of liminality is a powerful source of communal feeling in a context that goes beyond negation of ranking to a temporary irrelevance of all structure. Access to age peers under various conditions appears to promote social ties that provide both material and emotional benefits. In liminal circumstances, there may be, in addition, a spontaneous ferment of social creativity. Older people in many modern societies are exposed to all of these conditions. When peers are available, we should therefore expect that old people, like other people, will be linked to these age-mates in informal networks that provide both tangible and intangible support. Our surprise when we find these networks—and our slowness to look for them in the first place—are signs of the difficulty we have reminding ourselves that old people are indeed people.

Informal age bonds may in some circumstances and for some people be solidified into formal organizations focused in various ways on age. The conditions under which formal age associations appear, their internal structure, and the messages they direct toward the wider society are the subject of Chapter 6.

Chapter

6

Old Age
and Formal
Association

The most visible and dramatic usage of age in a social system is the distillation of age ideologies and informal networks of age association into formal age organizations. A formal age association is a group recognized by members and nonmembers as a social unit—it has a corporate "personality" and can make decisions, fight, or spend money as one entity. Such an association is also explicitly focused on age; it is not only recruited by age, but its purposes and activities are publicly defined as age-related. In sociological terms, a formal age association has a "manifest" function related to age, in contrast to many groups which may be age-homogeneous but whose functions are only implicitly or "latently" focused on age (Merton 1957, pp. 61–66).

The core questions for this chapter are the whys and wherefores of age association. When are more diffuse ideologies or more informal social contacts formalized into age associations? What are the consequences of the existence of age associations for their members, for other citizens in the same age category, and for the society at large?

Types of Formal Age Association
and Conditions Promoting Them

Formal age associations differ from one another inside and out—in internal structure and in the messages about age that they aim at the wider society. Age associations are likely to appear at points of asymmetry in insiders' and outsiders' attitudes toward age borders and their symbolic markers. Older and younger people may disagree about the rightness of old age being used to set some members of society apart in any way; they may also disagree about the attractiveness or usefulness of attributes that mark an individual as old (see Ross 1975, pp. 57–60 for general discussion of social borders and formal association). The different patterns of disagreement in evaluation of the existence of age borders and of their symbols produce the different goals and organizational styles of age associations.

For example, members of an organization may in effect *confess* having some shared characteristic in order to justify a demand on the wider society, or to find separate but parallel means to satisfy social needs that are difficult to meet outside. They may join a group to work with others like them to *erase* the identity they share, or, at the other extreme, to *emphasize* it.

An association which by its existence confesses the presence of a characteristic whose possessors do not value it positively is likely to result from asymmetry in attitudes of outsiders and insiders about its use to define a social border: those with the characteristic do not think it should be used to mark them off behind a border, outsiders do. An association that confesses a shared characteristic may make demands on the wider society, or may offer opportunities for friendship, recreation, or power not available to members in "mixed company." The California Institute of Social Welfare, founded in the 1940s by George McLain, is an example of the first type, as its main goal was to obtain higher pensions for old people with less bureaucratic humiliation (Pinner et al. 1959; Putnam 1970). Many "senior citizens" groups are examples of the second type. Although there is an age restriction on membership, their formal focus is often not on age but on various activities to which old people have little access in the wider society.

An association with the goal of erasing a border is likely to appear when individuals who share a characteristic value it positively but do not think it should be a basis for setting them apart, while outsiders think it should. Associations to erase a border are typified by ethnic organizations dedicated to assimilation or integration. Ethel Percy Andrus, founder of the National Retired Teachers Association and the American Association of Retired Persons, often expressed this kind of goal for old people who, she insisted, should not be treated like "basket cases." This type of organization usually wages a propaganda campaign to persuade outsiders that the border should be broken down, while at the same time meeting members' needs— for example, for inexpensive drugs, recreation, or transportation— until the goal is reached. Creation of an organization and develop-

ment of self-sufficiency often, of course, have the unintended consequence of making a border more visible to outsiders, more valued to
insiders, and consequently more likely to persist than to disappear.
For this reason, associations to erase a social border are often
forerunners of associations with the goal of border emphasis.

An association to emphasize a shared characteristic is likely to
result from the double asymmetry of a positive evaluation of both
border and marker by insiders and a negative evaluation of both from
the outside. Separatist ethnic organizations are examples of organizations that emphasize a border they feel should be maintained. The
Townsend organization, which gathered over two million old people
in the 1930s, was led by an old man who continually emphasized the
distinctiveness of old people as a category in the population, and
demanded respect and appreciation for their contribution to society.
Through his revolving pension plan, old people were, in addition, to
be the saviors of the depressed American economy (Holtzmann
1963).

The different messages of these different types of association are
typically carried by appropriately different types of leaders. The
association to confess grows out of negative attitudes toward a
characteristic by those who share it: they are likely to follow a leader
who is *not* like them. The integrationist goal of demonstrating that a
category of individuals who share a characteristic such as age should
not be set apart is more likely to support a leader who has the
characteristic—is old—but acts it out in ways most acceptable to
outsiders—is charmingly "spry." Emphasis on a border characteristic
requires a leader who shares it, but who also demonstrates its attributes in ways pleasing to insiders rather than outsiders: an old person
who looks old, identifies as old, stresses unique qualities of old
people, and probably acts unnervingly aggressive, sexy, or radical.

The old people as people theme reappears in the analysis of
associations around the age border, as both the factors promoting
various types of associations, and the strategies through which they
try to achieve their goals parallel those of associations based on other
social characteristics, such as ethnicity. The history of black associations in the United States, for example, shows the same progression
from confession to erasure to emphasis of the boundary that we will
trace for old age. Both the history of old-age associations in the
United States, and the traditional "gerontocracies" of East Africa and
Australia provide examples of these various types. The goals and
internal structure of these age associations, their leadership, and
their likelihood of success cluster in patterned ways around the
nexus of old people's and young people's evaluations and expectations of old age.

Although it is appropriate to discuss formal age association
mainly on a social level, the various types of organization have

implications on an individual level as well. The goals, structure, and leadership of a large, public association are visible—and audible—to the wider society. Their activities have consequences for the many old people who never join any group, both through tangible benefits they may achieve and through the more symbolic influence of the image they try to present. Israel's existence, for example, influences millions of Jews who never set foot there, and black power agitation had effects even on affluent suburban black Americans (Aberbach and Walker 1970).

The effects of age association on nonmembers are not hard to understand. Conditions that promote old people's participation in age-groups are much less clear. Both major interpretations focus on old age as a negatively evaluated characteristic. One argues that many old people will resist formal associations that require acknowledgement of the age identity. Resistance should logically be greatest from those with the most to lose—those old people who rank highest in terms of other social characteristics. Since it is known that those with higher class positions are more likely to participate in formal associations, this should severely limit recruitment. The other major view of recruitment into old-age associations starts from a similar premise, but leads to a different conclusion. Since inconsistency of statuses is often a motivation for participation in movements aimed at social change, those older people who have enjoyed higher achieved statuses should be more likely to join associations committed to improvement of the ascribed—and negative—status of old age.

Another of our central themes reemerges here: if old people are people, they are many different kinds of people. Analyses attempting to explain why all old people do or do not do anything are therefore inadequate from the start. If we match some major categories of old people with our various types of association, some of the apparent contradictions are untangled. The following descriptions of associations to confess an age identity suggest that old people with lower achieved statuses are their most likely recruits. Associations to erase age boundaries should be especially attractive to individuals suffering from status inconsistency. Age organizations to emphasize an age category are likely to be more varied in membership, as they are more variable in organizational structure.

Associations That Confess Old Age: The California Institute of Social Welfare

In a context where old age is generally negatively viewed, many old people may of course share that opinion themselves. They may, however, disagree strongly with younger people about whether old people should be treated differently from others. The old and young share attitudes toward age as a social characteristic, but disagree about its use as a basis of categorization. If power is in the hands of others, then an organization that "confesses" the negative attributes of old age and the existence of an age boundary may be a strategy for meeting needs that cannot be met otherwise precisely because of the age border imposed from the outside. Old people in California joined the California Institute of Social Welfare in the 1930s not because they were militants or because they though gray was beautiful, but because they wanted to escape the dependence caused by their low incomes. It was worth the risk of publicly "confessing" their old age by joining CISW in order to fight for higher state pensions without stigmatizing welfare requirements.

The old people who joined CISW wanted enough money to live as freely as they had when they were younger. Given their generally low evaluation of old age, it is not surprising that the person they turned to for leadership was not old himself. McLain was a younger man who said he would take care of his older supporters. As their "Uncle George," McLain sent members inspiration, counsel, and reports of his efforts on a daily radio show and in a monthly newspaper. The Welfare Service at the Los Angeles headquarters sent out letters and speakers to answer members' questions about the rights and problems of welfare recipients. In return, the members sent money to finance the office, the radio shows, and the lobbies in Sacramento and Washington. There was almost no intermediate organization. Information, encouragement, and requests for memberships and contributions came directly from McLain to the old people; their faith, dues, and donations went directly back to him. Local clubs were not emphasized in the early years of CISW, and they have never become very important. Most old people joined because of the radio show, and allegiance was to the central organization. Clubs that did form varied widely, depending on the previous organizational experience of their leaders: some were variations on an American Legion post; some resembled old-age fraternal orders. There was no interclub organization. CISW was essentially perpendicular in structure, with the relationship between the central figure and the supporters maintained by payments and services and expressed in a kinship metaphor. "Uncle George" would take care of his "old folks"; he needed their emotional and financial support to do it. This is the type of organizational structure often found early in associations of the relatively powerless (Wilson 1973). Members perceived the CISW as an association that did things *for* old people, not as a movement *of* the old (Pinner, Jacobs, and Selznick 1959; Putnam 1970; Pratt 1976).

CISW operated successfully as a lobby for old people in California except for one dangerously close brush with success. An organization whose goals and leadership derive from a dependent and negative definition of old age can appropriately ask for things from the wider society, but becomes suspect and threatening if it assumes a powerful stance and starts trying to tell younger people what to do. As supplicants asking through proper channels, and via a young spokesman, for a bit more support from society, members of CISW stayed close to current definitions of old age and appropriate social supports for the elderly. The association's greatest—and most appropriate—successes were placement of initiative proposals on the California ballot as formal requests from the old people to younger voters for bigger pensions and fewer humiliating bureaucratic hurdles to get them. In 1948, however, one of these initiatives included in its fine print the demand that the first state (as opposed to county) welfare director should be a CISW trustee. The immediate outrage of business groups and newspapers can be seen as a reaction strongly shaped by the negative view of old age built in to CISW itself. If old people were so dependent and needy, then the illogic of their acquiring power led to the conclusion that it was their leader who was power hungry. Suddenly property owners, PTAs, and civic associations were warned to "protect the needy" against George McLain. The initiative was repealed the next year, and McLain apparently never risked succeeding beyond expectations again. Although the anti-McLain propaganda had lingering effects, and no initiatives with his name attached were passed, several other welfare groups supported his general position and his followers granted him credit for pension increases which went through the legislature with more general backing.

CISW merged with organizations in Oregon and Washington in 1954, changed its name to National League of Senior Citizens in 1961, and continues to exist as a lobby, although "Uncle George" died in 1965. Partly as a result of its own efforts, however, CISW has been bypassed as changing expectations and supports from the younger society have provided a context where old people with more aggressive attitudes can organize without an "Uncle George."

An Association to Emphasize the Old-Age Border: Old Age Revolving Pensions, Inc.

CISW's threatening brush with success shows the sensitive connections among old people's attitudes and motivations, the structure of their association, and the expectations of the younger world outside. Another organization born in the fertile social incubator of Depression California makes the point even more firmly. McLain and his followers only stepped out of line once. Dr. Francis Townsend and his Old Age Revolving Pensions, Inc. attempted to redefine the line altogether. The OARP program did not simply ask for more money for the old, it made the old the financial saviors of the nation. Dr. Townsend's idea was to give every old person two hundred dollars a month, which had to be spent within that month, thereby stimulating production, providing jobs, and so on (the funds were to be raised by a transactions tax of 2 percent).

The organization Dr. Townsend created introduced an exuberantly positive purpose for association around age. Following their prophet, older people would lead the society out of economic chaos into prosperity. Depression desperation guaranteed almost any messiah at least a temporary audience; but OARP's one-man structure could not sustain support for a message that sounded too good to be true. OARP views of old age were in double disagreement with those of the younger society: old people had positive attributes and deserved a positive, permanent place as a social category whose age boundary might be emphasized by their contributions and directives to society at large. Official American attitudes still saw older people as a dependent, isolated social category. The formal action toward them was public assistance. It was no surprise to watch them flock into a mass organization, but the logic that expected them to be followers had to reject old people as an incongruous source of social change. If they were demanding money and claiming to save the world, someone must be manipulating them. Power over a perpendicular organization first brought Townsend to prominence as "a new Lincoln" and eventually exposed him to condemnation as "another Hitler" (see Downey 1936; Whiteman and Lewis 1936; Holtzmann 1963).

Early support for Townsend came loud and strong from both sides of the proposed age border. One hundred thousand copies of his organization's *Modern Crusader* newspaper sold out in southern California; circulation increased steadily and the paper spread to the north. Townsend spoke throughout the nation and attracted supporters as prominent as Frank Merriam, the Republican candidate who opposed Upton Sinclair and was later governor of California; author Kathleen Norris; Sheridan Downey, Sinclair's running mate; and the 110 congressmen who joined the "Congressional Townsend club." National headquarters was established in downtown Los Angeles; area and district managers were appointed to supervise the clubs which sprang up in the wake of the petition campaigns. These clubs were often vital social groups, but had no power over national policy or their own financial contributions.

Townsend and his colleague Earl Clements replaced the independently edited *Modern Crusader* with their own *Townsend Weekly*, which soon had a circulation of 150,000. In 1935, OARP, Inc. held a national convention in Chicago and experienced the respectable success of electing a declared Townsend advocate as a congressman from Michigan. The new official *Townsend Club Manual* prescribed a new and more detailed ladder of appointed offices from national headquarters, through regional headquarters, state, and district area headquarters to the local clubs. These were encouraged to canvas contributions and sponsor mass meetings and social events to send funds back up the ladder. By early 1936, Dr. Townsend reported receipts of $950,000. The momentum of faith and finances had reached a threshold: the old people had supported their prophet with a persistence that demanded a formal response from the surrounding society.

Official national discussion of the Townsend Plan began when the Seventy-fourth Congress opened its second session in January of 1936. Technically, the object of debate was California Congressman McGroarty's HR 7154, a bill endorsed by Townsend which asked for a 2 percent transactions tax whose proceeds would be distributed to all retired people over sixty. However, the discussion ranged across the abundance of specific proposals which had blossomed in the warm confusion of a crusade. Townsend's original petition demanded two hundred dollars a month for everyone who stopped working at sixty and urged a 2 percent transactions tax as the means to finance it. Later pamphlets did not specify the 2 percent, which economists attacked as insufficient; they asked instead for a tax large enough to finance the two-hundred-dollar pensions. In Senate Finance Committee hearings in 1935, Dr. Townsend was confronted with the incompatibility of a two-hundred-dollar monthly payment and a 2 percent tax which might bring at the most enough money to pay forty dollars a month. He suggested raising the eligibility age to sixty-five, seventy, or even seventy-five. Sheridan Downey revived this proposal in 1936 to try to reconcile economic critics to the plan. He proposed that the federal reserve bank buy a ten million dollar bond issue to pay the first pensions. Townsend wrote the preface to this book, and stated that he was "not irrevocably wedded to the transactions tax as the only method of raising money to finance the Townsend Plan" (Downey 1936, p. 10).

At this point, Townsend had changed the amount of pension in the McGroarty bill, the age of eligibility before the Senate Finance Committee, and the financial source in a book by Downey. The only unwavering essential the Townsend Plan presented for public debate was that age should define an age category with rights to income and to participation in social decisions. "Social dividends" recognized the mutual dependence—and equal worth—of the younger people seeking employment in the system of production and the older people seeking security beyond it. Recognition of their equal right to receive income and to participate in social change would benefit the entire society.

Although justifications varied with the specific plan, the negative judgment on this central proposal was swift and certain. Most Americans still considered old people a dependent and isolated group. The cure was surely not to give their situation legitimacy but to try to overcome it. The best answer to low incomes was not a permanent system of support for the nonproducers, but their return to production.

The second-best answer was support, carefully prorated according to each individual's previous production. This was written into the Social Security Act passed by the same Congress that defeated the McGroarty bill. If Social Security was in part a reaction against the Townsend Plan, the one element it adopted from OARP, Inc. became the root of a later reaction against the principle of Social Security. By accepting the Townsend use of age as the border between work and retirement, the original Social Security Act unintentionally reinforced age as a social boundary.

As we learned from CISW's one dangerous success, when a group's demands are incongruous with outsiders' expectations, the group's organizational structure becomes crucial. It can either persuade others that a dependent image is incorrect, or confirm it. One month after the House defeated the McGroarty "Townsend Plan" bill, it approved a congressional investigation of Dr. Townsend. When the perpendicular nature of OARP, Inc. was clearly exposed, it was not difficult to attribute the old people's unbecoming demands to their leader. Argument subsequently raged around Townsend and not his Plan. "The man who best of all Americans personifies the ideal democracy of which we have dreamed" became a "pseudo-Messiah, loudmouthed with Messianic complexes," and "strangely parallel to . . . Hitler" (Downey 1936, p. 23; Whiteman and Lewis 1936, pp. 265–66). At best he was a "good man with an idea, but misled." At worst the Townsend Plan was simply a means to feed Dr. Townsend (Whiteman and Lewis 1936, p. 118).

Witnesses reported Townsend's one-man management of OARP: his lack of intermediary controls over policy or money, his failure to report compromises and alliances to his members, his jealousy of emerging secondary leaders. He was publicly identified in support of the Union Party, as a peer of Father Coughlin and of Huey Long's "Share the Wealth" heir Gerald Smith—both already branded demagogues. Townsend's lieutenant resigned in an atmosphere of scandal aroused by accusations that he spent the old people's money on cars and clothes. Supporters of all ages began to fade away—radio announcers, member clubs, and state managers. Although Townsend placed one initiative on the California ballot in 1944, the voters defeated it. By the late forties, loss of both public prestige and appeal to the aging was complete.

A messiah with no followers has no leverage in the social order, and without the ability to move the power structure he has very little to offer believers. Townsend balanced briefly at the peak of a perpendicular organization which worked both ways. As the leader of two and a half million voters, he was assured an audience in Congress; and his influence in Washington convinced the members that he was carrying their message.

As soon as the politicians could detach Townsend from the old people he claimed to serve they could justify not listening to him, and when the politicians stopped listening, old people had little reason to join the crusade. If OARP, Inc. had risen in a steady hierarchy from members to director, weakening the organization would have been more difficult. Because there was no intermediate power, however, there was only one man to be discredited. Whether Dr. Townsend was rejected as opportunistic or deluded, he was no longer accepted as the voice of two and a half million voters. And without a voice to shake the nation, he could not keep the old people behind the Plan.

OARP, Inc. was an association that *emphasized* old age, accepting it as a positive social identity and stressing what old people had to offer as well as what they needed. Appropriately, their leader was himself an old man. However, the organization's internal structure was inconsistent with the positive definition of old people as appropriate social participators; and the external evaluations of old age were more consistent with the dependent structure than with the assertive message. CISW members did not like being behind an age boundary, but confessed its existence to get support they needed; OARP supporters emphasized that from their distinctive vantage they could give the rest of the society good advice. A second generation of old-age associations in America brought still another message about old age as a social border—their goal was to *erase* it.

The Integrationists: NRTA-AARP

The employment needs of World War II brought American old people brief and false rejuvenation by removing many younger men from the labor force. After the war ended, however, retirement settled back into place as a social boundary, national interest turned back to domestic affairs, and a new kind of history began for old-age organizations.

This history follows a slow, steady growth in strength, which only very gradually accumulated the force to turn the attention of old-age associations back toward changes in their society. The energetic search for problems and solutions kept the new organizations essentially self-centered until they eventually came to the limit of self-analysis, where perception of problems outweighs the power to change. At this point they had to ask the surrounding society for help. They had by this time, however, developed an internal organization solid enough to support a request from strength instead of weakness. In fact, their most urgent request was for the one thing they could never achieve alone—recognition of their new strength.

The National Association of Retired Civil Employees and the National Retired Teachers Association were established in 1947. Their names announce that at this cautious new beginning for age association, age was not even allowed to stand alone as a principle of recruitment; its use as a source of social identity was bolstered by common occupation. The members of these organizations had no experience with being dependent; they were not interested in hiring a broker or in following a messiah. As former teachers and civil servants, they were used to forming groups and committees to get things done. They directed most of their attention toward themselves; and what they wanted from the wider society, they elected representatives to request. Both NARCE and NRTA asked first for more money; and they have continued to submit "respectfully urged" requests for improved retirement incomes. In the process of presenting these requests, however, both organizations discovered many more needs and a surprising self-sufficiency in meeting them.

The National Retired Teachers Association was willed into existence by one person with one angry concern; but membership and interests rapidly multiplied. When Ethel Percy Andrus retired as principal of a California high school, she was shocked into action by the size of her first pension check. After simmering inconclusively around the state legislature for several months, she decided that retired teachers needed a national organization, and by 1947 NRTA was in existence and attracting dues-paying members at one dollar a head.

When the new members tried to decide what to do with their time and money beyond requesting better retirement pay they began counting the curses of old age. The priority was unanimous: retired people needed protection against the expense of sudden accidents and lingering illness. Insurance was almost impossible for anyone over sixty-five, since most policies were either cancelled or shifted to a prohibitively high premium level when their holders reached that age.

Dr. Andrus began a siege of the insurance companies, and soon learned the painful extent of confusion between the physical effects and the social definitions of age. She represented a group of people placed by their age in a new social category. The insurance companies showed her studies of health and life expectancy based on old people in hospitals. They generalized the most negative physical effects of age to everyone in the new social sector it defined. Dr. Andrus insisted that she had never been in a hospital and that "the insurance companies' trouble was that they just didn't meet any healthy old people." After several persistent years, she convinced Leonard Davis of Continental Casualty to try. They wrote NRTA members a noncancellable, inexpensive group policy with monthly payments and no physical examination.

Continental discovered that retired teachers lived moderately, took good care of themselves medically, and drove cautiously: they were ideal insurance risks. The retired teachers discovered that by accepting "retired" as a group identity they could get what they wanted from society. The twin discoveries that (1) self-sufficiency was possible if (2) it could be communicated to the wider society directed the development of a new kind of old-age organization.

So many nonteachers tried to smuggle their way into the National Retired Teachers Association insurance program that in 1958 Dr. Andrus formed the American Association of Retired Persons to make group insurance available to anyone over fifty-five. For AARP, disagreement with the younger society was again double, but in a new pattern. Because they saw old age as a positive life stage, AARP members felt they should *not* be set apart. The aim of AARP was to "offer senior Americans a chance to solve their own problems of personal identity, recreation, travel, health protection, and financial security."

Modern Maturity magazine brought members information, inspiration, and news about themselves. They began to contact each other and form local clubs, where they continued to count the curses of retirement in America. Their discussion lengthened the list of retirement dilemmas, which in turn dictated new departments for the national organization: travel services, discount mail-order pharmacies, Institutes of Lifetime Learning, hospitality lounges, retirement residences, preretirement magazines, counselling services to industries and government agencies, consumer information centers, a research and welfare association, a radio program, state directors and area vice-presidents, and annual regional and national conferences.

The one major problem which was not immediately susceptible to AARP's energetic do-it-yourself approach was the attitude of younger Americans toward retirement. Members therefore worked not only to be self-sufficient, but worked to let everybody know about it. Like the CISW, they have not made major efforts to change the structure of society (e.g., AARP was not a strong supporter of Medicare); but like the Townsendites, they want a positive place in it. Unlike either, their requests are in the present; they do not want recognition for past achievements, but for their present position.

The one demand AARP members have most persistently presented to other Americans is for recognition of their consistent *lack* of demands: "America's elderly are neither indigent nor childlike, but are responsible, self-serviceable folk, eager to solve their own problems and to help others, both young and old, to solve theirs. Their testimony is that they find old age a rewarding segment of life." As in most associations aimed at erasure of a social boundary, AARP's original leader was a person who embodied the positive aspects of old age from the point of view of the *outside* society. Dr. Andrus was in these terms a "spry" old lady, attractive to younger people because of her similarities to them, not because of her distinctive qualities as an older person. African nationalists with British accents, or women executives in tailored suits use similar strategies. Like many other integrationist associations, AARP combines "insiders" and "outsiders"—old people with young—in its leadership and management roles. Younger people work as lobbyists and hold the more managerial positions; the president of the association is an old person. In this way, AARP is closer to CISW than to the Townsend movement, although there is a significant role shift from "Uncle George" as caretaker to the AARP staff as employees. The internal structure of an association with an integrationist goal must also be consistent: members must participate, they must do things for themselves, and their demands to the wider society should be for an end to discrimination, but not for support or radical social change.

Townsend's movement to emphasize positive aspects of an age identity was, as we have seen, ahead of its time. Development of associations like AARP has laid the foundations for another far more successful round of militant age organizations. Moderate integrationist associations often have this unexpected side effect. By organizing to make themselves *less* distinctive, and to demonstrate that lack of difference to the world at large, integrationists often persuade themselves that they do have positive things in common, and make their commonalities more visible to the others. This unexpected development builds a good foundation for a type of association that *emphasizes* the common identity, old age.

Once again, militant old people emerge as leaders, but this time backed up by participatory organizations addressing a wider society apparently more ready to accept the old as activists.

Associations That Emphasize Old Age:
AARP, NCSC, Gray Panthers

When individuals believe both that a characteristic they share has positive aspects and that it is appropriate for them to behave and to be treated in some distinctive ways because of those characteristics, then if they group together formally, their goals will be more militant and their premise in communication with outsiders will be their permanent and positive place in the society. Instead of joining together to erase the age boundary, they will emphasize it.

Changes within AARP itself represented some shift from erasure to emphasis of the old age boundary. During approximately its first decade, AARP was squarely within the definition of an integrationist organization. More recently, both its increased use of resources for lobbying and its strong links to government agencies and to legislators represent a shift toward emphasis rather than erasure of an age boundary: retired people are being represented as a permanent and positive segment of the population. AARP is still a moderate association, however, and is not dedicated to radical social change. Its twelve million members tend to be from white-collar backgrounds, and services provided by AARP to its membership are still the mainstays of its recruiting and financial base. Much of its lobbying and provision of information to decision makers continues to stress a more positive image for the old rather than specific material benefits.

The National Council of Senior Citizens came into being as an association to emphasize old people as a distinctive category, and has the characteristics of this kind of organization more sharply defined. The Council grew out of the Senior Citizens for Kennedy group formed during the 1960 election campaign. It sprang from an activist, partisan political orientation, and continued in that style when Aimé Forand, as a retiring congressman, officially organized NCSC to continue his fight for medical insurance for the elderly. NCSC was vigorously involved in the battle to pass the Medicare bill, and most observers agree that the association did play a significant role in that victory. Its position on Medicare to begin with qualifies NCSC as an association that emphasizes old age as a social boundary. Because Medicare uses federal dollars to offer coverage to almost all old people regardless of their work history, this support is justified in terms of the special needs of a distinctive social category, not by previous individual contributions to production.

NCSC has survived both the transition to new leadership and the transition to new issues. It continues to have tight links to labor unions, and to put relatively more of its resources into lobbying than into services to members, although insurance, drugs, travel, and so on are offered. The focus of NCSC lobbying is more material than symbolic, with particular stress on improved income levels. NCSC is also consistently more willing than AARP to demand deeper social changes in order to provide more financial security for old people—for example, more use of general revenue to support Social Security, thus detaching it from previous productivity and justifying income more forthrightly on the basis of membership in an age category.

Gray Panthers are the newest and the most vocal of the associations that emphasize the age border—the name says it all. Or almost all, since the border these militant old people emphasize is not, as in the other cases, that between the old and everyone else. Gray Panthers attempt to ally the young and the old against discrimination from those at the power fulcrum of the middle years. The name Gray Panthers was invented jokingly by the media for the "Consultation of Older and Younger Adults for Social Change" organized by Maggie Kuhn in 1970. The group of about one hundred took on the militant name officially a year later. As the Panthers have grown to a membership of over 50,000 they have continued to emphasize the common problems of young and old: job discrimination, drug abuse, exclusion from decision making. Panthers demonstrate, picket, and lobby for better health care for the elderly, fairer representation of old people by the media, adequate housing via rent control and regulation of condominium conversion, and abolishment of mandatory retirement. Panthers have also published exposés and handbooks on topics such as hearing aids and nursing homes (Clearwater 1981). Although some of their antiageist rhetoric sounds as though the Panther goal is to erase age boundaries, their efforts seem directed rather at asserting rights to recognition and participation for young and old—but mainly old—who are *not* just like everyone else, but who have unique qualities that could improve the entire society.

Reminiscent of Townsend? All these associations around an emphasized age border share something of his message to the wider society: old people are not like everyone else, but that should have positive rather than negative implications. The old do demand rights and assert needs, but social change required to accomplish these will benefit the entire society. Further, the old in these associations are ready to specify those changes and to participate in their implementation.

The differences from Townsend's movement are more significant than the similarities to it, since it is the differences that explain how AARP and NCSC have surpassed Townsend in both longevity and respectability.

The warmer reception of old-age associations in political arenas, like anything to do with social borders, has two sides. The old people themselves are organized differently and there have also been changes in the wider political scene. Both AARP and NCSC have survived their separation from founding leaders. They have both developed internal structures of participation that can support claims to positive participation in the society outside. In addition, of course, they both have the history of earlier associations behind them, as Townsend did not. The well-publicized self-sufficiency message of early AARP backs up all of these more emphatic associations. Townsend and the other earlier militant leaders also provide a reminder of the vehemence that an old person's movement can muster and the kind of comparative radicalism that often makes more moderate associations more acceptable by contrast. The Gray Panthers may offer some of this good cop–bad cop effect in the present day, as a desire to avoid their militance may make decision makers more willing to deal with AARP and NCSC. It is too early to know whether the Gray Panthers will survive their charismatic leader and founder Maggie Kuhn. The prognosis seems to be good; there is a national network of Panther groups with 50,000 members.

Another significant change inside the age border is population increase. The dramatically greater number of old people—and widely publicized expectations of even more—obviously offers greater leverage to associations that can claim to represent even a segment of this expanding category of voters.

There are changes outside the old-age boundary too. Many signs of increasing age consciousness are present and intensifying: in popular media, professional associations, legislative structures, government agencies, professional and popular books. In addition, since the early 1960s interest groups are interpreted by many political scientists as an increasingly effective avenue to influence. A major strategy available to old people seems to be becoming more acceptable at the same time as their numbers raise the salience of old-age issues both to the public and to decision makers.

What happens in the long run to associations that emphasize an identity—what would winning mean? Achievement of recognition that old age is and should be a positive and permanent category in the population and on the political scene is a plausible definition of victory. If enough is won, the next type of association old people should create is one to *maintain* an age boundary. The dramatic successes of recent old people's associations may lead to a new kind of organization that protects position rather than demanding it.

Associations to maintain a social boundary such as age arise when those who share a characteristic value it positively and want to protect its use as a border from others who would like to break down the social fences and share in the benefits. Credential or licensing organizations represent this type of association; so do parties or groups dedicated to preservation of ethnic or gender privilege. Although old people in the United States have certainly not yet reached the status of a privileged category that might associate in order to protect that position, great gains in both financial support and symbolic recognition have been made by the old—and are now being threatened by new federal policies toward programs such as Medicare and Social Security. When we consider the possibility that old-age associations may need to begin working to maintain, rather than expand, old people's access to resources, the elders of traditional gerontocracies may have some practical advice to offer.

Associations to Maintain an Age Border: Gerontocracy

The most outstanding fact about gerontocracies is that most of them do not exist. If we define gerontocracy in the way most of us usually think about it, it means a political system in which old people hold the power. Unless we are willing to call the United States a gerontocracy, this must mean more than that some old people occupy high political positions. If we use the narrower definition that a gerontocracy exists when all old people, because of their age, have all the political power, we are talking about a rare phenomenon. The purest or strongest type of gerontocracy has been called *ascribed* gerontocracy. In contrast is the much more common pattern of *achieved* gerontocracy, in which most power is held by the old because various channels to power, such as accumulation of cattle or land, or marrying many wives, are more accessible to the old than to the young. Skillful negotiation of many marriages is such a widespread basis for uneven power distribution between old and young that one anthropologist has invented the label "gerontogamy" to replace gerontocracy in these cases (Almagor 1978b). The key difference between ascribed and achieved gerontocracy is that in one case being old is a guarantee of greater access to power, in the other it only offers a headstart.

Old men among the Tiwi of Australia are excellent examples of the opportunities available to wily gerontogamists. In this hunting and gathering band, the secret of prosperity is womanpower. The more women a man has in his household, the more food supplies he can accumulate, and the more he can redistribute as a means to prestige. Since a successful career of polygamy takes many years of careful strategy, it is old men who have the most wives—and consequently most children—in their households. But not all old men are successful. Although only the old have had time to exchange sisters for brides, sire daughters, exchange daughters for brides, and marry widows throughout enough years to create large and prosperous households, not all men use their years or their female connections as shrewdly. The clearest evidence that if the Tiwi have a gerontocracy it is achieved, not ascribed, comes from the unfortunate individuals who have only years, but not sisters or daughters, to their credit (Hart and Pilling 1960, esp. pp. 51–78).

East Africa is the heartland for the rarer cases of ascribed gerontocracy. Among the Samburu of northern Kenya, the oldest men belong to a senior generation set which has both political and ritual power. The distribution of scarce resources in favor of the older men is similar to that among the Tiwi. In these East African communities, however, the older men's advantage is formalized through the age organization. Younger men are not allowed to marry until they reach a certain stage in the ladder of age-grades, usually in their thirties. The elders are believed to control a powerful curse, which gives them a ritual authority over the younger men.

The Samburu elders are, in our terms, an association that maintains an age boundary. Anthropologists who have unraveled the complexities of many age systems point out that it is most likely gerontocracy that leads to age-sets, and not vice versa. The older men who have preferential control over stock, wives, and political decisions use symbolic means, like curses and rituals, to maintain their resource advantage: "Sets give open expression, cognitive order, and ritual respectability to the velvet-gloved hand of the aged with which they wield their control of productive resources" (Baxter and Almagor 1978, p. 19). Another way to contrast the Tiwi and the Samburu is to say that the older Samburu are successfully using ascription to rationalize their achieved advantages.

Is it too optimistic to wonder whether older Americans might ever need an association to maintain an age boundary? Might they achieve enough benefits to need to protect them with an organization based on their common ascriptive status of old age? Older Americans already need this type of association, in my opinion, although for rather more pessimistic reasons. I predict some shift of direction in existing associations toward maintenance or protection of benefits already acquired, as debates about new federal policy raise fears about Social Security, Medicare, and many other social supports. If we follow through the comparison with the traditional elders then we should expect a greater use of symbolic strategies in old people's politics. Although, given our cultural context, any cursing done by the old is likely to be both private and fairly ineffective, other ritual and symbolic techniques are available. Organized groups with some privileged access to tangible resources often use a smokescreen of powerful symbols to protect it. General references to fairness, equal-

This Boran (Kenya) man is respected for his position in a senior age-grade and for his expertise in astronomy. (Photo by Asmarom Legesse)

ity, or the American way are not good ways to acquire resources from a political system, but they may do any excellent job of maintaining or protecting them (Edelman 1964 and 1971). Broad, symbolic appeals are not the right way to approach decision makers, since they elicit broad, symbolic responses. If you ask for "more rights," you're likely to get a Commission on Rights. However, a flurry of symbols directed to the wider public may effectively camouflage more specific tangible and private demands to authorities: invocation of national defense is a smokescreen for lucrative weapons contracts.

We can expect increased use of emotional public messages, made in ascriptive terms—in the name of all elderly—while lobbying continues behind the scenes. The veteran who fought for us, the discrimination of mandatory retirement, the previous lifetimes of hard work, even the mother who made us apple pie are likely to appear in justification of maintained support for older Americans. The Gray Panthers' media watches and their reports of prejudicial imagery for older characters are an early step in this direction.

As long as a financial squeeze at federal levels creates threats to both tangible and symbolic benefits—resources and the social identities required for access to them—maintenance of an age border is likely to be an important basis for association. When or if previous gains seem more secure, older Americans, like other political actors, will be less likely to subside than to associate more emphatically (Edelman 1964).

Conclusion

Old people appear as people in the political arena as well as in more private domains. The various styles and levels of formal age association have been explained with reference to general theories of social movements, social border definition, and political organization. We don't need a special theory of old people's politics, because they operate politically much like anyone else. The point needs emphasis only because there is a perhaps wishful tendency to think that they do not—that is, that they will not organize in pursuit of their own interests. Debate takes place among gerontologists about whether old people's associations should be seen as interest groups or social movements (Binstock and Hudson 1976, pp. 383–84). Depression period organizations are considered irrelevant to present political analysis because of the special characteristics of that historical moment. The many loyalties and identities of elder individuals other than age are described as obstacles to any broadly age-based political mobilization. What does all this say about old people to make them different from other political actors? They have many social identities, each of which may ascend to priority for political action at various times; and these identities, such as age, ethnicity, and occupation, are likely to be combined in the recruitment patterns of formal associations. They live in a historical moment, with particular types and levels of stress that may or may not promote different kinds of collective action by various types of individuals or members of various social categories.

None of this adds up to the conclusion that age is not relevant to politics in our society. It does underscore the extent to which old people must be viewed, like any other political actors, as influenced by individual experience, historical period, and cultural context. The question is not whether age is politically salient for all old people all the time, but for which old people, under what conditions, manifested how?

Older Americans are not only the objects of governmental policy, in their well-publicized role of social problems; they have also been creators of political change. The old have also influenced major social policies, such as Medicare. Recent age associations and responses to them rest on the foundation of earlier old people's actions. In the short run, future old people's associations are likely to worry about holding on to the benefits they have gained. Although they have not won enough to be in a league with the gerontocratic elders of East Africa, some of the protection strategies perfected there might be useful. Younger Americans should expect to be the audience for a proliferation of public and symbolic messages justifying—or temporarily obscuring—special benefits to the old as an ascriptive category.

Much speculation has been spun out over the longer-term future of old people's associations. Some of the bases for prediction have to do with particular characteristics of the old in the United States; others grow out of the "old people are people" theme and the abstract features of various types of associations. The numbers and proportions of old people are increasing, which in turn increases their public visibility and salience. Their educational level is increasing also, and with it the likelihood of various kinds of political participation. Old people in the future will also have reached old age through years spent in a different atmosphere of attitudes toward age: age will have been more culturally and politically salient and explicit throughout their lives (Cutler 1981).

These age-specific changes are all reasons why formal association based on age should continue or increase. The more abstract arguments made in this chapter about sources and types of association also lead up to a prediction that age association should continue in the United States. Since disagreement about evaluation of age as a social border, its symbolic markers, or both is the requisite for association, we would have to expect a dissolution of those disagreements to see the end of age associations. In the very long run, this might happen, but in the more visible future the question seems to be not whether there will be formal age associations, but what kind.

Chapter

7

Mapping the Human Experience of Aging

The Cultural Context

At this point we have the specifics from people and places around the world to fill in the implications of viewing old people as people and old age as a human phenomenon.

What do we gain by stressing the humanness of old age? First, the most distinctive feature of humans is our cultural adaptation. Far more than any other animal, we create a filter of patterns and meanings which defines the environment—physical, social, and cognitive—in which we live. We are cultural creatures. The implication for old age is that its experiences will be conditioned by the patterns and meanings of a particular culture. The aging process or the situation of old people cannot be understood without reference to its cultural context. The entire map of age differentiation must be charted in a particular setting before we can make sense out of either physical or social aspects of being old.

Second, culture is transmitted socially. Unlike many other animals, most of our "design for living" must be learned, and transmitted from generation to generation. Human infants are extremely helpless not only physically, but also socially: we require tremendous support for a long time before we are capable of full participation in a human social group. Studies of other primates also show how unusual humans are in the amount of social support they share throughout their lives. Monkeys only need that intensive social support—and only get it—in infancy; humans require social bonds throughout life, and are exceedingly ingenious at creating and maintaining them against the most improbable odds.

An old man in Texcoco Plaza (Mexico) represents the challenges posed for the elderly by rapid social changes such as urbanization. (Photo by Jay Sokolovsky)

What are the implications of human sociability for old age? If the cultural side of human life emphasizes its variability, the social side highlights the universal. Humans are social creatures, and acquire their indispensable cultural maps through participation in social groups. The extent of their interdependence in a social context is unique among primates. Old people everywhere need continued patterned connections to the web of social relationships surrounding them. If either the norms for what these connections ought to be, or the actual opportunities to play them out, are absent, we should expect the old people as members of the ingenious human species to create and discover them. If social participation is absolutely impossible, we should not be surprised if culturally sanctioned death results.

The old people are people theme has implications not only for what old age is, but also for how we study it. The cultural variability of aging experiences, combined with the early acquisition and all-encompassing quality of culture as a filter for experience, warns us that it will be difficult to extricate a scientific vantage point from the comfortable confines of our own culture's definitions of age and aging. Awareness of cross-cultural diversity is also a reminder of diversity on the individual level. The extent of variation in life careers is itself variable across cultures. Culture is a filter, not a rigid template. Because cultural maps are learned and used by individuals, there is always some individual difference in experience, although the range of difference that may be publicly tolerated varies from one society to another. In addition, the cultural map itself inscribes categorical differences: the categories of individuals defined as distinct are likely to have correspondingly various life experiences. Since the categories given social significance are not universal, the American tendency to lump all old people into a homogeneous category may obscure our view of individual diversity in other societies as well as in our own.

Old people are people also says that like all humans, they are actors, not just passive receptacles into which cultural directives are poured. Cultures and societies change, and the agents are human. The perceptions, feelings, and responses of human actors perpetually shape the cultural definitions and social situations that in turn influence those responses. The attribution of passivity to the old is another American tendency that must not be generalized as part of a scientific approach to old age.

The Dimensions of Age Differentiation

The harshest description of American cultural definitions of old age is that they do not treat it as a human condition. A scientific approach to understanding age must begin by restoring an assumption of humanity for the old. From that assumption flow the basic premises that experiences of aging are culturally shaped, and played out in a social context; that old people are diverse, both as categories in various societies, and as individuals; and that the old have the potential to be active, creative forces in their cultural and social contexts. The dimensions of age differentiation used to structure the chapters of this volume are one way to map the human experience of aging around the world. Along each dimension the strands of basic human experience intertwine: culture, sociability, diversity, invention.

The Cognitive Dimension

That life courses come in many various shapes and sizes is the first cross-cultural lesson; the second lesson is that what a life course looks like is more or less culturally relevant in different communities. "The long graying line" refers to a middle-aged and medicalized American view of the life span, which we must restrain ourselves from imposing on human lives everywhere. A life that follows one line into inevitable and irrevocable loss and decline is not a universal notion. Life may continue after death, in the sense that an individual's role in the community may if anything intensify after physical death. The line may bend into a circle, as the oldest age-grade is joined by—or recycled into—the most junior. Life may indeed be viewed as a line, but one ascending into power and ritual activity rather than descending into passivity. Or there may be many lines if distinct careers are perceived in various domains such as reproduction, ritual, and subsistence; individuals may age differently, may progress through careers differently in various domains. The shape and direction of the life course have clear implications for how individuals feel about progressing through it. The cultural relevance of the entire life course as a unit for prescription and evaluation also has consequences for the social aspects of aging, in particular for the definition of support for the old in terms of reciprocity versus dependence.

Cultural distinctions inside the life span also affect the way old people are linked to other members of their communities. As the two similar Sudanese tribes of Mesakin and Korongo demonstrated, the number of age-grades sliced across the life span affects the congruity between physical capacity and social age, and consequently the relations across generation borders. The Eskimos and the ice floes are the extreme case of another consequence of cognitive categories within the life course. When the old are subgrouped into either intact or decrepit, there is a possibility of social participation, high status, and good treatment for one category of old people in the same community that abandons, kills, or doesn't support old people in the other category. This double vision of the old should be food for thought in a culture that includes a seventy-year-old president on the one hand, and a substantial number of malnourished institutionalized old people on the other.

The White House versus the nursing home for Americans of similar chronological age also raises the issue of how age is defined or measured, and with what consequences. Although chronological age is given more prominence in some cultures than others, recent United States surveys show that functional attributes are still highly significant in modern settings. Physical anthropologists remind us how variable are the requirements—and the permissible supports—for functionality in different cultures. The fact that a seventy-year-old person in the White House does not imply excellent social and physical circumstances for all elderly stems from another classification issue. President Reagan did not acquire power on the ascriptive basis of his age, as a Samburu elder does. If anything, he achieved the presidency in spite of his age, which he rather carefully minimizes: his seventieth birthday party was virtually a state secret. Conversely, there is a double whammy awaiting the many older Americans who cannot avoid loss of significant achieved identities, and must deal with faceless categorization by the ascriptive criterion of old age.

The inventiveness characteristic of humans facing new environmental demands also appears along the cognitive dimension of age. The rituals of transition used in most human communities to guide people across the uncharted territory between defined social statuses are not available for old people in many modern settings. These old people both need the rites of passage and invent them.

The Normative Dimension

Human ingenuity is a prominent characteristic of older people's invention of norms. Many observers have pointed out that the newness of an extended life stage between work and death has left it relatively normless. One of the most dramatic findings about communities of the old is their normative creativity. It is also true that on an individual level, we all engage constantly in smaller scale norm creation. We don't follow norms as if they were a railway schedule, but negotiate and haggle with others in social situations, and tinker with our society's guidelines for conduct. Older people as individuals, in all their daily encounters, are carrying on this smaller scale norm creation as well. Since less is well defined for them, there is a larger element of creativity in their negotiations, but the fundamental process is the same.

The norms created by older people among themselves are parallel to those of age-groups in many traditional societies. Egalitarian emphases are strong, probably because age similarity is an excellent metaphor for equality among an out-of-power group in a hierarchical context. The insulating qualities of egalitarianism are fiercely defended by age-mates from Samburu to Les Floralies. Normative creativity also produces rules for coping with basic human issues such as sex, death, and physical and emotional support. The social scaffolding all humans need to work through these experiences is provided by peers through a network of reciprocity that does not require admissions of dependence. Although the invention of ritual responses to death, "health-protectors," in-house marriages, and so on has been reported most extensively in old-age communities, we do not know that they occur only there. Since we do know that people of all ages do better in stressful situations if they have the safety net of a strong social network, a significant avenue for new research is into the conditions and consequences of peer ties among old people in the natural settings where by far the majority live.

Norms also evoke the cultural and social aspects of human behavior. These shoulds and oughts are strongly influenced by the values in a cultural context; and of course their purpose is to guide social interaction. Because they involve interaction among individuals and categories of people, norms also remind us of human diversity. The vehemence of American evaluation of dependency, for example, has a strong inhibiting effect on older people's willingness to accept support of any kind from their children; in China, an old person can glory in filial care. As we have seen, the result in the United States is considerable disagreement between old and young about what children's responsibilities ought to be. The enforcement of norms requires a social setting where the young-old interaction is both visible and salient, requirements which will be increasingly met in many American communities.

The Ideological Dimension

An age bias that focused studies of age ideology exclusively on the young has only recently been overcome. The same principles invoked to explain an emphasis of age borders among the young account for the emergence of "generational units" in old age. Change that is rapid, but not so fast that it blurs social differences, promotes awareness of cohort distinctiveness. Certain types of change are schismogenic—they trigger more differentiation across a social boundary such as age. Both the rate and the types of social change in recent American experience should promote age ideologies. These are apparent on the more intimate level of institutions and local communities, as well as projected on the larger scene of national policy.

Ideology and conflict are usually discussed in the same breath, but ideology and explicit age differentiation do not necessarily produce conflict. Conflict is a basic human activity, not necessarily destructive, and certainly not reserved for the young. General social theories—not special old people theories—have been used to produce hypotheses about conditions promoting age conflict. Social ties that cross-cut the age boundary should reduce conflict across it. Since, in the United States, alternative social demands and loyalties are fewer in adolescence and old age, these should be the age-grades most likely to develop conflictual relations with those in the middle. Explicit age organization may emphasize age differences, but relieve the intensity of conflict by channeling it into more institutionalized modes such as elections, lobbies, or legislative debate. Spatial separation in relation to age conflict is itself a controversial topic. Anthropologists and the people with whom they have worked in Africa and Latin America see separation of age-groups in space as a means of conflict avoidance; American social observers have been more likely to see separate residence as a source of conflict. Although some of the difference may be due to variations in the distances involved, what we know about age-homogeneous communities of old people so far reveals them to be more like the "good company" of Nyakyusa. Strains on particular intergenerational relations seem to be eased by the availability of a more ritualized and collective level to which tension can be shifted as necessary.

The Interactional Dimension

Old people also "vote with their feet" for various patterns of age differentiation, as they choose friends and develop connections with informal networks. The most visible results of older people's informal association are of course the communities they have created. The old people are people theme is central here, as the old-age communities have been created in response to the same factors that stimulate community creation among squatters, nation-builders, and utopians. The communities are also a response to the essential human need for sociability. Inventiveness is abundantly displayed in the social worlds that develop inside these new communities: age, sex, and ethnicity take on new meanings; ethnic rituals or political identities are "recycled" into new, present-tense patterns. Old people are human with a vengeance when it comes to fighting for their view of what the new community should be. Although the factional battles typical of new communities for the old are a major annoyance to administrators, they are a mark of success in creation of a setting in which old people can create a community they care enough to fight about. As we saw, it is the newness—rather than the old age—of these settings that stimulates community conflicts. Relative lack of definition combined with acutely felt lack of alternatives are conducive to a fight.

Since a very small proportion of old people live in separate residences, it is important to trace informal social networks outside them. In this domain, we have far more theory than fact. General social theories of homophily, role strain, liminality, stereotyping, stigmatization, and response to threat all produce propositions in the

An American grandfather and grandson act as sidewalk superintendents. The alliance of old and young may be an important source of change in American age relations. (Photo by Jennie Keith)

same direction: that older people in most American communities are likely to find many important social satisfactions among peers. The diversity caveat is still present, of course. Individuals are varyingly exposed to conditions such as stigma or threat. They are also variously "sensitive" to the availability of peers, depending, for example, on how many roles they have lost, whether they are men or women, and how old they are. Who is identified as a peer in the first place also varies with the age identity that an older person assigns herself or himself.

Like many other informal domains of human social life, such as the worlds of women in most societies, the informal lives of old people are little known in any cultural context. We still have much to learn from our elders: it will take many hours of listening and watching before we understand the meaning of age in the hours and days of informal activity that make up most of our social lives.

Formal Age Association

When ideology or informal socializing is distilled into formal association, our central themes reappear: old people are as humanly social, cultural, diverse, and inventive as ever. Formal associations around the age border arise out of the social dialogue across the boundary. Asymmetry in evaluations of the age border itself and/or of its symbolic markers produces the formal associations. The exact content of this social-level "conversation" shapes the internal structure and external aims of each organization. The cultural context also provides both resources and constraints for age associations, which in turn stimulate changes in cultural values and social structures. American perceptions of the old as passive and dependent had important implications for the public response to early organizations such as the California Institute of Social Welfare or the Old Age Revolving Pensions, Inc. American ambivalence about explicit acknowledgement of any social differentiation also continues to place additional constraints on any associations that emphasize an age boundary. Certainly there is still a tendency for many decision makers to feel more comfortable treating the elderly as social problems rather than social participants. National associations such as AARP and NCSC, however, *are* successfully participating in information collection, agenda setting, and decision making. Regardless of the specific outcomes on particular issues, that participation should have reverberating implications for perceptions of older Americans. The diversity in types of old-age associations is matched by diversity of responses from old people, ranging from participation in different associations and at different levels of involvement to no participation at all.

Conclusion

Where does our map of age differentiation lead us? In general, away from attempts to generalize about all old people, or the aging process, either worldwide or within one society; toward awareness of the mutual influence of old people and their social and cultural context, of the diversity among old people, and of their potential to be active, creative social participants. In the United States in particular, what we can put on the map of age differentiation so far suggests that it will increase. Although we may shift toward an age-irrelevant society in the long run, the very battlelines drawn in attempts to achieve it will emphasize age boundaries in the near future.

The one universal statement we should permit ourselves about old age is that it is a part of the human experience, perhaps even a uniquely human experience. A major contribution of cross-cultural consideration of old age should be the conclusion that future research and action can begin—rather than end—with the discovery of old people as people.

References

Aberbach, J., and Walker, Jack. "Political Trust and Racial Ideology." *American Political Science Review* 64 (1970): 1199–1219.

Alger, Johanna F. *Activity Patterns and Attitudes toward Housing of Families in Specially Designed Apartments for Aged in Ten New York City Projects.* Ithaca, N.Y.: Cornell University Housing Research Center, 1959.

Almagor, Uri. "Equality among Dassanetch Age-Peers." In *Age, Generation, and Time,* edited by P. T. W. Baxter and Uri Almagor. London: Hurst, 1978a.

———. "Gerontocracy, Polygyny, and Scarce Resources." In *Sex and Age as Principles of Social Differentiation,* ed. J. S. LaFontaine. London: Academic Press, 1978b.

Amoss, Pamela. "Religious Participation as a Route to Prestige for the Elderly." In *Dimensions: Aging, Culture and Health,* ed. Christine L. Frey. New York: Praeger (a James Bergin Book), 1981.

Apple, Dorian. "The Social Structure of Grandparenthood." *American Anthropologist* 58 (1956): 656–63.

Bateson, Gregory. "Culture Contact and Schismogenesis." In *Beyond the Frontier,* edited by Paul J. Bohannan and Fred Plog. Garden City: Doubleday, 1967.

Baxter, P. T. W., and Almagor, Uri. Introduction to *Age, Generation, and Time,* edited by P. T. W. Baxter and Uri Almagor. London: Hurst, 1978.

Beall, Cynthia. "Theoretical Dimensions of a Focus on Age in Physical Anthropology." In *Age and Anthropological Theory,* edited by David Kertzer and Jennie Keith. Forthcoming.

Becker, Gaylene. *Growing Old in Silence.* Berkeley: University of California Press, 1980.

Bengtson, Vern, and Cutler, Neal. "Generations and Intergenerational Relations: Perspectives on Age Groups and Social Change." In *Handbook of Aging and the Social Sciences,* edited by Robert H. Binstock and Ethel Shanas. New York: Van Nostrand, 1976.

Binstock, Robert H., and Hudson, Robert B. "Political Systems and Aging." In *Handbook of Aging and the Social Sciences,* edited by Robert H. Binstock and Ethel Shanas. New York: Van Nostrand, 1976.

Blau, Zena Smith. "Structural Constraints on Friendship in Old Age." *American Sociological Review* 36 (1961): 429–39.

Bultena, Gordon. "Structural Effects on the Morale of the Aged: A Comparison of Age-Segregated and Age-Integrated Communities." In *Late Life: Communities and Environmental Policy,* ed. Jaber F. Gubrium. Springfield, Ill.: Charles C. Thomas, 1974.

Bultena, Gordon, and Powers, Edward. "Age-Grade Comparisons and Adjustment." In *Time, Roles, and Self in Old Age,* ed. Jaber F. Gubrium. New York: Behavioral Publications, Inc., 1976.

Burgess, Ernest. "Personal and Social Adjustment in Old Age." In *The Aged in Society,* ed. Milton Derber. Urbana: University of Illinois Press, 1950.

Byrne, Susan. "Arden, an Adult Community." In *Anthropologists in Cities,* edited by George Foster and Robert Kemper. Boston: Little, Brown, 1974.

———. "Arden, an Adult Community." Ph.D. dissertation, University of California, Berkeley, 1971.

Carp, Frances. "Housing and Living Environments of Older People." In *Handbook of Aging and the Social Sciences,* edited by Robert Binstock and Ethel Shanas. New York: Van Nostrand, 1976.

Clark, Margaret. "Cultural Values and Dependency in Later Life." In *Aging and Modernization,* edited by Donald Cowgill and Lowell D. Holmes. New York: Appleton-Century-Crofts, 1972.

Clark, Margaret, and Anderson, Barbara. *Culture and Aging: An Anthropological Study of Older Americans.* Springfield, Ill.: Charles C. Thomas, 1967.

Clearwater, C. *Gray Panther History: 1970–1981.* Philadelphia: Gray Panther National Office, 1981.

Cohen, Carl, and Sokolovsky, Jay. "Social Engagement vs. Isolation: the Case of the Aged in SRO Hotels." *The Gerontologist* 20, no. 1 (1980): 36–44.

Coleman, James. *Community Conflict.* New York: Free Press, 1957.

Cool, Linda E. "Role Continuity or Crisis in Later Life: A Corsican Case." *International Journal of Aging and Human Development* 13, no. 3 (1981): 169–181.

———. "Ethnicity and Aging: Continuity through Change for Elderly Corsicans." In *Aging in Culture and Society,* edited by Christine L. Fry. New York: Praeger (a James Bergin Book), 1980.

Cowgill, Donald. "Modernization: A Revision of the Theory." In *Late Life: Communities and Environmental Policy,* edited by Jaber F. Gubrium. Springfield, Ill.: Charles C. Thomas, 1974.

Cowgill, Donald, and Holmes, Lowell, eds. *Aging and Modernization.* New York: Appleton-Century-Crofts, 1972.

Cutler, Neal. "Political Characteristics of Elderly Cohorts in the Twenty-First Century." In *Aging: Social Change,* ed. Sara B. Kiesler. New York: Academic Press, 1981.

Davis, Kinglsey. "The Sociology of Parent-Youth Conflict." *American Sociological Review* 5 (1940): 523–34.

Dolhinow, Phyllis. "The Primates: Age, Behavior, and Evolution." In *Age and Anthropological Theory,* edited by David Kertzer and Jennie Keith. Forthcoming.

Downey, Sheridan. *Pensions or Penury.* New York: Harper, 1939.

———. *Why I Believe in the Townsend Plan.* Sacramento: Sheridan Downey, 1936.

Durkheim, Emile. *The Division of Labor in Society.* Translated by George Simpson. New York: Free Press, 1933.

Eckert, J. Kevin. *The Unseen Elderly*. San Diego: Campanile Press, 1980.

Eckert, J. Kevin, and Beall, Cynthia. "Approaches to Measuring Functional Capacity Cross Culturally." In *New Methods for Old Age Research*, edited by Christine L. Fry and Jennie Keith. Chicago: Center for Urban Policy, Loyola University of Chicago, 1980 (2nd expanded edition. New York: Praeger, 1982).

Edelman, Murray. *Politics as Symbolic Action: Mass Arousal and Quiescence*. Chicago: Markham, 1971.

––––––. *The Symbolic Uses of Politics*. Urbana: University of Illinois Press, 1964.

Eisenstadt, Shmuel N. *From Generation to Generation: Age Groups and Social Structure*. New York: Free Press, 1956.

Elder, Glen. "Age Differentiation and the Life Course." *Annual Review of Sociology*, vol. 1. Palo Alto: Annual Reviews, Inc., 1975.

Epstein, William. *Politics in an Urban African Community*. Manchester: Manchester University Press, 1958.

Erickson, Rosemary, and Eckert, J. Kevin. "The Elderly Poor in Downtown San Diego Hotels." *The Gerontologist* 17 (1977): 440–46.

Evans-Pritchard, E. E. *The Nuer*. London: Oxford University Press, 1940; rpt. 1968.

Fel, Edit, and Hofer, Tamas. *Proper Peasants: Traditional Life in a Hungarian Village*. Chicago: Aldine, 1969.

Fennell, Valerie. "Older Women in Voluntary Organizations." In *Dimensions: Aging, Culture, and Health*, ed. Christine L. Fry. New York: Praeger (a James Bergin Book), 1981.

Feuer, Lewis S. *The Conflict of Generations*. New York: Basic Books, 1969.

Foner, Anne. "The Polity." In *A Sociology of Age Stratification*, edited by Matilda White Riley, Marilyn Johnson, and Anne Foner. Aging and Society, vol. 3. New York: Russell Sage Foundation, 1972.

Francis, Doris Goist. "Adaptive Strategies of the Elderly in England and Ohio." In *Dimensions: Aging, Culture, and Health*, ed. Christine L. Fry. New York: Praeger (a James Bergin Book), 1981.

Frank, Gelya. "Life Histories in Gerontology: The Subjective Side to Aging." In *New Methods for Old Age Research*, edited by Christine L. Fry and Jennie Keith. Chicago: Center for Urban Policy, Loyola University of Chicago, 1980 (2nd expanded edition. Praeger, 1982).

Friedman, Edward P. "Age, Length of Institutionalization, and Social Status in a Home for the Aged." *Journal of Gerontology* 22 (1967): 474–77.

Fry, Christine. "Structural Conditions Affecting Community Formation Among the Aged." In *The Ethnography of Old Age*, ed. Jennie Keith. Special Issue of *Anthropological Quarterly* 52, no. 1 (1979): 7–18.

––––––. "The Ages of Adulthood: a Question of Numbers." *Journal of Gerontology* 31 (1976): 170–77.

Gelfand, Donald E. *Aging: The Ethnic Factor*. Boston: Little, Brown, 1982.

Gessain, Monique. "Les classes d'Age chez les Vassari d'Etyolo." In *Classes et Associations d'Age en Afrique de l'ouest*, ed. Denise Paulme. Paris: Plon, 1971.

Giallombardo, Rose. *Society of Women*. New York: John Wiley and Sons, 1966.

Gibbs-Candy, Sandra E. "A Developmental Exploration of the Functions of Friendship in Women." Paper presented to the 29th Annual Meeting of the Gerontological Society, 13–17 October 1976, in New York.

Glascock, Anthony, and Feinman, Susan. "Social Asset or Social Burden: an Analysis of Treatment of the Aged in Non-Industrial Societies." In *Dimensions:*

Aging, Culture, and Health, ed. Christine L. Fry. New York: Praeger (a James Bergin Book), 1981.

————. "Toward a Comparative Framework: Propositions Concerning the Treatment of the Aged in Non-Industrial Societies." In *New Methods for Old Age Research,* edited by Christine L. Fry and Jennie Keith. Chicago: Center for Urban Policy, Loyola University of Chicago, 1980 (2nd expanded edition, 1982).

Goffman, Erving. *Stigma: Notes on the Management of Spoiled Identity.* Englewood Cliffs, N.J.: Prentice-Hall, 1963.

Gross, Neal; Mason, Ward; and McEachern, Alexander. *Explorations in Role Analysis: Studies of the School Superintendency Role.* New York: Wiley, 1957.

Gubrium, Jaber F. *Living and Dying in Murray Manor.* New York: St. Martin's Press, 1975.

Guemple, D. L. "Human Resource Management: The Dilemma of the Aging Eskimo." *Sociological Symposium* 2 (1969): 59–74.

Gulliver, Philip. "Age Differentiation." *International Encyclopedia of the Social Sciences* (1968). New York: Free Press.

————. *Social Control in an African Society.* London: Routledge and Kegan Paul, 1963.

Gutmann, David. "Alternatives to Disengagement: The Old Men of the Highland Druze." In *Culture and Personality: Contemporary Readings,* ed. Robert LeVine. Chicago: Aldine, 1974.

————. "Aging among the Highland Maya." In *Middle Age and Aging,* ed. Bernice L. Neugarten. Chicago: University of Chicago Press, 1968.

Harlan, William H. "Social Status of the Aged in Three Indian Villages." *Vita Humana* 7 (1964): 239–52. (Reprinted in *Middle Age and Aging,* ed. Bernice L. Neugarten. Chicago: University of Chicago Press, 1968.)

Hart, C. W. M., and Pilling, A. R. *The Tiwi of Northern Australia.* New York: Holt, Rinehart and Winston, 1960.

Hendel-Sebestyen, Giselle. "Role Diversity: Toward the Development of Community in a Total Institutional Setting." In *The Ethnography of Old Age,* ed. Jennie Keith. Special Issue, *Anthropological Quarterly* 52 (1979): 19–28.

Hess, Beth. "Friendship." In *A Sociology of Age Stratification,* edited by Matilda W. Riley, Marilyn Johnson, and Anne Foner. Aging and Society, vol. 3. New York: Sage, 1972.

Hill, Jennie Keith. *The Culture of Retirement.* Ph.D. dissertation, Northwestern University, 1968.

Hochschild, Arlie. *The Unexpected Community.* Englewood Cliffs, N.J.: Prentice-Hall, 1973.

Hoestetler, J. A., and Huntington, Gertrude. *The Hutterites in North America.* New York: Holt, Rinehart and Winston, 1967.

Holtzmann, Abraham. *The Townsend Movement.* New York: Bookman Associates, 1963.

Howell, Nancy. *The Demography of the Dobe !Kung.* New York: Academic Press, 1979.

————. "Toward a Uniformitarian Theory of Human Paleodemography." In *The Demographic Evolution of Human Populations,* edited by R. H. Ward and K. M. Weiss. London: Academic Press, 1976.

————. "An Empirical Perspective on Simulation Models of Human Population." In *Computer Simulation in Human Population Studies,* edited by B. Dyke and J. W. MacCluer. New York: Academic Press, 1974.

Hrdy, Sarah Blaffer. " 'Nepotists' and 'Altruists': The Behavior of Old Females among Macaques and Langur Monkeys." In *Other Ways of Growing Old,* eds. Pamela Amoss and Stevan Harrell. Stanford: Stanford University Press, 1981.

Hudson, Robert B., and Binstock, Robert H. "Political Systems and Aging." In *Handbook of Aging and the Social Sciences,* edited by Robert H. Binstock and Ethel Shanas. New York: Van Nostrand, 1976.

Hughes, Charles C. "The Concept and Use of Time in the Middle Years: The St. Lawrence Island Eskimo." In *Aging and Leisure,* ed. Robert W. Kleemeier. New York: Oxford University Press, 1961.

Johnson, Sheila. *Idlehaven: Community Building Among the Working Class Retired.* Berkeley: University of California Press, 1971.

Jonas, Karen. "Factors in Development of Community in Age-Segregated Housing." In *The Ethnography of Old Age,* ed. Jennie Keith. Special Issue of *Anthropological Quarterly* 52 no. 1 (1979): 49–60.

Kandel, Randy, and Heider, Marion. "Friendship and Factionalism in a Tri-ethnic Housing Complex in North Miami." In *The Ethnography of Old Age,* ed. Jennie Keith. Special Issue of *Anthropological Quarterly* 52 no. 1 (1979): 29–38.

Katz, Solomon. "Anthropological Perspectives on Aging." *Annals of the American Academy of Social and Political Science* 438 (1978): 1–20.

Kayser-Jones, Jeanie. *Old, Alone and Neglected: Care of the Aged in Scotland and the United States.* Berkeley: University of California Press, 1981.

Keith, Jennie. "The Best is Yet to Be: Toward an Anthropology of Age." *Annual Review of Anthropology, Vol. 9.* Palo Alto, CA: Annual Reviews, Inc., 1980a.

———. "Old Age and Community Creation." In *Aging, Culture and Society,* ed. Christine L. Fry. New York: Praeger (a James Bergin Book), 1980b.

———. "Participant Observation." In *New Methods for Old Age Research,* edited by Christine L. Fry and Jennie Keith. Chicago: Center for Urban Policy, Loyola University of Chicago, 1980c (2nd expanded edition. New York: Praeger, 1982).

———. ed., *The Ethnography of Old Age.* Special Issue of *Anthropological Quarterly* 52 no. 1 (1979). (See also Ross, Jennie Keith).

Kertzer, David. "Generation and Age in Cross-Cultural Perspective." In *Aging from Birth to Death: Sociotemporal Perspectives,* ed. Matilda White Riley. Boulder, Colo.: Westview Press, 1981.

Kertzer, David, and Madison, Oker B. B. "Women's Age Sets among the Latuka of Sudan." In *Dimensions: Aging, Culture and Health,* ed. Christine L. Fry. New York: Praeger (a James Bergin Book), 1981.

Kiesler, Sara B. "The Aging Population, Social Trends and Norms of Behavior and Belief." In *Aging: Social Change,* ed. Sara B. Kiesler. New York: Academic Press, 1981.

Laufer, Robert S., and Bengtson, Vern. "Generations, Aging and Social Stratification: On the Development of Generational Units." *Journal of Social Issues* 30 (1974): 181–206.

Legesse, Asmarom. "Age Sets and Retirement Communities." In *The Ethnnography of Old Age,* ed. Jennie Keith. Special Issue of *Anthropological Quarterly* 52 no. 1 (1979): 66–69.

———. "The Controlled Cross-Cultural Test." *Ethos* 1 (1973a): 522–30.

———. *Gada.* New York: Free Press, 1973b.

Lowenthal, Marjorie Fiske; Thurner, Madja; and Chiriboga, David. *Four Stages of Life.* San Francisco: Jossey-Bass, 1975.

Lowie, Robert. "Societies of the Sidatsa and Mandan Indians." *Anthropological Papers of the American Museum of Natural History* 11 (1913): 219–358.

Lozier, John, and Althouse, Ronald. "Social Enforcement of Behavior toward Elders in an Appalachian Mountain Settlement." *The Gerontologist* 14 (1974): 69–80.

Mannheim, Karl. "The Problem of Generations." In *Essays on the Sociology of Knowledge,* ed. Karl Mannheim. London: Routledge and Kegan Paul, 1952.

Marshall, Victor W. "Socialization for Impending Death in a Retirement Village." *American Journal of Sociology* 80 (1975): 1124–1144.

Maxwell, Robert, and Silverman, Philip. "Information and Esteem." *Aging and Human Development* 1 (1970): 361–92.

Maybury-Lewis, David. "Aging and Kinship: A Structural View." In *Age and Anthropological Theory,* edited by David Kertzer and Jennie Keith. Forthcoming.

———. *Akwe-Shavante Society.* Oxford: Clarendon Press, 1967.

Mead, Margaret. *Culture and Commitment: A Study of the Generation Gap.* Garden City, N.Y.: Doubleday, 1970.

Merton, Robert. *Social Theory and Social Structure,* rev. ed. New York: Free Press, 1957.

Middleton, John. *The Lugbara.* New York: Holt, Rinehart and Winston, 1966.

Mitchell, J. Clyde. *The Kalela Dance: Aspects of Social Relationships among Urban Africans in Northern Rhodesia.* Rhodes-Livingstone Paper no. 27. Rhodes-Livingstone Institute, 1956.

Moore, Sally Falk. "Old Age in a Life-Term Social Arena." In *Life's Career-Aging: Cultural Variations on Growing Old,* edited by Barbara Myerhoff and Andrei Simic. Beverly Hills: Sage, 1978.

Moss, Miriam; Gottesman, Leonard; and Kleban, Morton. "Informal Social Relationships among Community Aged." Paper presented to the 29th Annual Meeting of the Gerontological Society, 13–17 October 1976, in New York.

Myerhoff, Barbara. *Number Our Days.* New York: Dutton, 1978.

Nadel, S. F. "Witchcraft in Four African Societies." *American Anthropologist* 54 (1952): 18–29.

NCOA (National Council on Aging). *The Myth and Reality of Aging in America.* Washington, D.C.: National Council on Aging, 1976.

Needham, Rodney. "Age, Category and Descent." In *Remarks and Inventions,* ed. Rodney Needham. London: Tavistock, 1974.

Neugarten, Bernice, and Hagestad, Gunhild. "Age and the Life Course." In *Handbook of Aging and the Social Sciences,* edited by Robert Binstock and Ethel Shanas. New York: Van Nostrand, 1976.

Neugarten, Bernice; Moore, Joan W.; and Lowe, John. "Age Norms, Age Constraints, and Adult Socialization." *American Journal of Sociology* 70 (1965): 710–17.

Neugarten, Bernice, and Peterson, Warren. "A Study of the American Age-Grade System." *Proceedings of the International Association of Gerontology* 3 (1957): 497–502.

Ottenberg, Simon. *Leadership and Authority in an African Society: The Afikpo Village-Group.* Seattle: University of Washington Press, 1971.

Palmore, Erdman and Manton, K. "Modernization and Status of the Aged." *Journal of Gerontology* 29, no. 2 (1974): 205–10.

Paulme, Denise. "Blood Pacts, Age Classes and Caste in Black Africa." In

French Perspectives in African Studies, edited by Pierre Alexandre. London: Oxford University Press, 1973.

Pinner, Frank A.; Jacobs, Paul; and Selznick, Philip. *Old Age and Political Behavior: A Case Study.* Berkeley and Los Angeles: University of California Press, 1959.

Plath, David W., and Ikeda, Keiko. "After Coming of Age: Adult Awareness of Age Norms." In *Socialization and Communication in Primary Groups,* edited by Thomas R. Williams. The Hague: Mouton, 1975 (Distributed by Aldine).

Pratt, Henry J. *The Gray Lobby.* Chicago: University of Chicago Press, 1976.

Press, Irwin, and McKool, Michael. "Social Structure and Status of the Aged." *Aging and Human Development* 3 (1972): 297–306.

Putnam, Jackson K. *Old Age Politics in California: From Richardson to Reagan.* Stanford: Stanford University Press, 1970.

Radcliffe-Brown, A. R. "Age Organization Terminology." *Man* 29 (1929): 21.

Ragan, Pauline, and Dowd, James. "The Emerging Political Consciousness of the Aged." *Journal of Social Issues* 30 no. 3 (1974): 137–58.

Riley, Matilda; Johnson, Marilyn; and Foner, Anne. "Age Strata in Society." In *Aging and Society,* eds. Matilda Riley, Marilyn Johnson, and Anne Foner. New York: Russell Sage Foundation, 1972.

Rose, Arnold. "The Subculture of the Aging." In *Middle Age and Aging,* edited by Bernice Neugarten. Chicago: University of Chicago Press, 1968.

Rosenberg, George. *The Worker Grows Old.* San Francisco: Jossey-Bass, 1970.

Rosenmayer, Leopold, and Köckeis, Eva. "Family Relations and Social Contacts of the Aged in Vienna." In *Social and Psychological Aspects of Aging,* vol. 1, edited by Clark Tibbitts and Wilma Donahue. New York: Columbia University Press, 1962.

Rosow, Irving. "What is a Cohort and Why?" *Human Development* 21 (1978): 65–75.

———. "Status and Role Change Through the Life Span." In *Handbook of Aging and the Social Sciences,* edited by Robert H. Binstock and Ethel Shanas. New York: Van Nostrand Reinhold, 1976.

———. *Socialization to Old Age.* Berkeley: University of California Press, 1974.

———. *Social Integration of the Aged.* New York: Free Press, 1967.

Ross, Jennie-Keith (Keith, Jennie). *Old People, New Lives: Community Creation in a Retirement Residence.* Chicago: University of Chicago Press, 1977 (paperback edition, 1982).

———. "Learning to Be Retired: Socialization into a Retirement Residence." *Journal of Gerontology* 29 no. 2 (1975a): 211–23.

———. "Social Borders: Definitions of Diversity." *Current Anthropology* 16 (1975b): 53–72.

Schurtz, Heinrich. *Alters Klassen und Männerbunde.* Berlin: Reimer, 1902.

Shanas, Ethel. "The Family as a Social Support System in Old Age." *The Gerontologist* 19, no. 2 (1979): 169–74.

Shanas, Ethel, et al. *Old People in Three Industrial Societies.* London: Routledge and Kegan Paul, 1968.

Sherman, Susan. "Patterns of Contacts for Residents of Age-Segregated and Age-Integrated Housing." *Journal of Gerontology* 30 (1975): 103–7

Simmons, Leo. *The Role of the Aged in Primitive Society.* New Haven: Yale University Press, 1945.

Skinner, William. "Intergenerational Conflict among the Mossi." *Journal of Conflict Resolution* 5 (1961): 55–60.

Sokolovsky, Jay, and Cohen, Carl. "Being Old in the Inner City: Support Systems of the SRO Aged." In *Dimensions: Aging, Culture and Health,* ed. Christine L. Fry. New York: Praeger, 1981.

————. "The Cultural Meaning of Personal Networks for the Inner City Elderly." *Urban Anthropology* 7 (1978): 323–42.

Southall, Aidan. "The Illusion of Tribe." In *The Passing of Tribal Man in Africa,* ed. Peter Gutkind. Leiden: E. J. Brill, 1970.

Spencer, Paul. "Opposing Streams and the Gerontocratic Ladder: Two Models of Age Organization." *Man* 11 (1976): 153–74.

————. *The Samburu: A Study of Gerontocracy in a Nomadic Tribe.* London: Routledge and Kegan Paul, 1965.

Stewart, Frank. *Fundamentals of Age-Group Systems.* New York: Academic Press, 1977.

Talmon, Yonina. "Aging in Israel, A Planned Society." In *Middle Age and Aging,* ed. Bernice Neugarten. Chicago: University of Chicago Press, 1968.

Teaff, J. D.; Lawton, M. Powell; and Carlson, D. "Impact of Age Integration of Public Housing Projects upon Elderly Tenant Well-being." *The Gerontologist* 13 (1977): 77–81.

Terray, Emmanuel. "Classes and Class Consciousness in the Abron Kingdom of Gyaman." In *Marxist Analyses and Social Anthropology,* ed. Maurice Bloch. New York: Wiley, 1975.

Trela, James. "Status Inconsistency and Political Action." In *Time, Roles, and Self in Old Age,* ed. Jaber F. Gubrium. New York: Behavioral Publications, 1976.

Trela, James, and Sokolovsky, Jay. "Culture, Ethnicity and Policy for the Aged." In *Ethnicity and Aging,* edited by Donald Gelfand and D. Fandetti. New York: Springer, 1979.

Turner, Victor. *The Ritual Process.* Chicago: Aldine, 1969.

Van Arsdale, Peter. "Disintegration of the Ritual Support Network among Aged Asmat Hunter-Gatherers of New Guinea." In *Dimensions: Aging, Culture and Health,* ed. Christine Fry. New York: Praeger (a James Bergin Book), 1981.

————. "The Measurement of Age." In *New Methods for Old Age Research,* edited by Christine L. Fry and Jennie Keith. Chicago: Center for Urban Policy, Loyola University of Chicago, 1980 (2nd expanded edition. New York: Praeger, 1982).

Wellin, Edward, and Boyer, Eunice. "Adjustments of Black and White Elderly to the Same Adaptive Niche." In *The Ethnography of Old Age,* ed. Jennie Keith. Special Issue of *Anthropological Quarterly* 52, no. 1 (1979): 39–48.

Whiteman, Luther, and Lewis, Samuel L. *Glory Roads: The Psychological State of California.* New York: Crowell, 1936.

Whiting, John M.; Kluckhohn, R.; and Anthony, A. "The Function of Male Initiation Ceremonies at Puberty." In *Readings in Social Psychology,* edited by Eleanor Maccoby, T. Newcomb, and E. Hartley. New York: Holt, Rinehart and Winston, 1958.

Whyte, William Foote. *Street Corner Society: The Social Structure of an Italian Slum.* Chicago: University of Chicago Press, 1955.

Wilson, James Q. *Political Organizations.* New York: Basic Books, 1973.

Wilson, Monica. *Good Company: A Study of Nyakyusa Age Villages.* London: Oxford University Press, 1951.

Young, Frank, and Bacdayan, A. "The Function of Male Initiation Ceremonies: A Cross-Cultural Test of an Alternative Hypothesis." *American Journal of Sociology,* 67 (1962): 379–96.

Index